I Know Why They Call a Shell a Shell:

Tales of Love Lost at Sea

By Hayley Rose Horzepa

I Know Why They Call a Shell a Shell:

Tales of Love Lost at Sea

Hayley Rose Horzepa

Copyright 2013

Published by Hayley Horzepa

ISBN-13: 978-1470104351

A special thanks to SJH

This book is dedicated to all women

who survived domestic violence

as well as the ones who did not

and

to all the dolphins and marine animals that died

as a result of the BP Gulf Oil Spill in 2010

I

Ophelia

I did love you once-

One bitter Vermont morning, I awoke to find the windows smashed out of my truck and scattered all over my boyfriend's driveway. This was merely the result of my latest abusive relationship. The night before, I slept over his house. That morning, when he broke the news to me about the windows, he did an awful job of acting surprised. Nor did he offer me any assistance in cleaning up the mess. Instead he got dressed, went to work, and left me alone to pick up the pieces.

Glass crunched under my sneakers as I walked up to my truck. Clutching a few black garbage bags in one hand and a metal dustpan in the other, I stared at the driver's side window. Large sections of tempered glass still clung to its frame. Like thin ice before cracking, fissures spread out in every direction, and held together for one last unforgettable moment; the last thing one sees before falling through. This was not the only object of mine a boyfriend would destroy. Although my windows were never touched again, my heart often became a more than willing casualty.

It was not the first time he let me down. The year before, we took a road trip across the country. After less than a week of exploring the US, we found ourselves on Virginia Beach, Virginia. Little did I know that during that afternoon of sand and shore, the day's record heat would give me the worst sunburn I'd ever experienced.

As we carelessly lounged in the sand, he spoke of childhood vacations he took to the beach with his family. They often vacationed there out of convenience. His father was military pilot and the lodging was practically free when they stayed at the Air Force Base. On those trips, they would wake up early and go to the beach to see wild dolphins swim by the shore in pods.

My eyes lit up at the thought. Dolphins? I pictured a candy-colored sunrise reflecting onto the ocean's shimmering surface as the graceful mammals swam down the shoreline. I had spent most of my life inland in New England where I was fluent in the language of fall foliage and winter storms; never before had I seen a dolphin in the wild, nor considered doing so a possibility.

As the long summer day faded into early evening, my skin started to glow a rosy hue; an aura that soon covered my entire body. It was not long before I felt like a piece of burnt toast, dry and crispy. To make matters worse, we were camping *in a tent*. It was pretty late when we finally got back to the campground.

I tried to sleep. Despite my best efforts, I could not ignore the feeling of the abrasive sleeping bag material as it rubbed against my seething skin. To take my mind off the discomfort, I focused on our plans for the following morning: to get up at sunrise so we could catch a glimpse of the wild dolphins.

"Are you alright, Hayl?" He must have noticed me wriggling uncomfortably beside him.

"I can't sleep. My skin is burning."

"You probably just need some aloe."

"Aloe? Where do you get aloe? Honestly, I don't feel like going anywhere right now..."

"Don't worry about it. I'll go get it," he said then abruptly stood up, threw on his pants and left. I stared at the dark tent's vinyl ceiling and listened to the truck's engine fade away until it was replaced by the sound of silence. Silent it was. We were not deep enough in the woods to hear crickets, nor close enough to the ocean to hear waves.

Twenty minutes passed and he had not returned. I began to wonder what was taking him so long but tried to rest and keep my mind off of it. *Then twenty minutes turned into forty.* I dialed his number on my cell, but he did not pick up the phone. I dialed his number again. No answer. He quickly called me back.

"Why didn't you pick up when I called you?" I pried.

"Sorry, I didn't hear it ringing. I was driving and had the radio on loud. "

"Where are you?"

"I'm leaving the store right now, I'll be back in ten minutes."

"What's taking you so long?" I demanded.

"Gotta go, bye," he hung up.

Another hour passed. Finally, he returned to the tent with aloe and excuses. He said that he was gone for so long because he could not find aloe anywhere. *How stupid of me.* I should have anticipated that it would take him almost two hours to find aloe on a location like Virginia Beach.

It was more likely that he had so much trouble finding the aloe because he was looking for it in a bar. He was a bad alcoholic and probably pounded several pints while he was gone. The next morning, he refused to get up at sunrise like we had planned. I poked him and pleaded for him to wake up so we could go to the shore. *I so badly wanted to see the dolphins.* He just grumbled and turned away from me.

We eventually made it to the beach; it was just much later in the day than I expected. At the beach, we walked along what seemed like an endless boardwalk. I stared out to the sea and closely scrutinized the crest of each wave for fins. There were plenty of waves, but no fins. After an hour of this, we decided to give up, but then my boyfriend announced that he saw one.

"You saw one?" I exclaimed. "Where?"

Now I surveyed the waves frantically.

"Oh, it's gone now" he smirked,"but it was...ummm...over there!" He said and pointed indiscriminately out to sea.

I looked in the direction of which he pointed. Aside from and endless queue of waves lining up to hit the shore, nothing was to be seen.

"Why didn't you point it out to me?" I was so disappointed.

He laughed at my question. His laughter made me even more upset than I already was. It seemed that even this response amused him further.

Not only had I still never seen a dolphin in the wild, but now, I had *almost* seen one and missed it. This new predicament was much worse than never seeing a wild dolphin to begin with. The joy he derived from my pain made me bitter and set the tone for the rest of our six-week journey.

It was no surprise he left that morning without offering to help me clean up the glass. I was tired and disoriented. I swept just enough glass off the driver's seat to enable me to drive the truck to the gas station. Before I could go anywhere, I had to remove the remaining shards that clung to the window frame. I used the plastic brush handle to knock them off the door. With one of the black garbage bags, I tried unsuccessfully to catch the pieces as the they rained to the ground like tears.

Sweeping the glass off the driveway with the ancient dustpan proved to be equally challenging and made deep scraping noises with each stroke. I finally finished, wrapped up and disposed of the bags. On my walk back to the truck, little glimmers caught my eye. Near my truck, part of his lawn was sparkling. There would be no more sweeping on my part. I pretended not to notice, and got into the vehicle.

As I drove, remnants of glass pinched my butt through my jeans. The floor too was covered with tiny shards. Even the steering wheel was sprinkled with nearly invisible slivers of glass so small that I never would have discovered them had they not become imbedded in my palms.

Windowless, I drove to the gas station where I made a phone call to my insurance company. As luck would have it, my policy did not cover glass. At this point, I was just grateful that they did not break my windshield. I pulled up to the enormous vacuum cleaner. With ease, it devoured the large piles of glass from the seats and floor. Afterwards, I went back to my boyfriend's house. I sat pensive like Rodin's *Thinker* as I tried to figure out who did it. *He* was with me the entire night, *I was his alibi.*

His friends, the likely culprits, would not admit to anything. All of them played dumb. One of them was on probation and had a girlfriend who was an enabler. When the police went to his apartment to question him, she told them that he had been with her and had not left the house the entire night.

The whole story was suspicious. The previous morning, I was awoken by my car alarm beeping softly. These quiet beeps were meant to alert me the car had been tampered with. *How strange,* I thought. Who would mess with my car in the middle of the rural Vermont? *Surely something was wrong with the alarm itself.*

I told my boyfriend and he suggested that I leave the alarm off the following night so my faulty alarm system would not wake up the entire neighborhood, should it go off again. Things felt too coincidental the next morning when I discovered my windows in pieces all across his driveway. Still, he insisted that his friends were innocent.

When he got home from work that night, I waited for him to jump in the shower so I could go through his phone. At first everything seemed innocuous. There were no texts between he and his friends that mentioned the planning or enactment of such an event. I did, however, find something that I was not looking for.

There was a disproportionate amount of texts between him and his brother. Upon closer investigation, I noticed the texts were made up of sexual comments and flirtation. My eyes widened. After looking through his phone and then his Facebook, I soon realized he had been having a relationship behind my back with an 18-year old college student. He saved her number under his brother's name to further deceive me, should I ever look through his cell's contents. On Facebook I found out that the girl was a college cheerleader. I began to wonder if maybe her and her cheerleader friends were responsible for my shattered my windows.

I panicked and went through my phone and Facebook. I scrambled to find a friend who lived in the area, someone who's place I could go to before he got out of the shower. I could not stay another night with my soon to be ex-boyfriend, but at the same time, I could not make the drive back to Connecticut without windows. It was March and far too cold to do that. Not to mention, the windows I ordered from a local mechanic had not yet arrived.

Though I had spent most of the afternoon calling every glass place in the phonebook, I could not find anyone who could help me that day or even the next. They were *all* on *Vermont time*. It would take three days minimum for my new windows to come in.

I texted a close college friend, who lived nearby. He lived with his parents, but had the house to himself that entire week. He graciously offered me a spare room where I could hide out for as long as I needed to.

That afternoon, it became clear that the young cheerleader was not at all to blame for my broken windows. My phone rang. It was my boyfriend's friend. He offered his assistance and said he was going to look for and possibly buy me replacement windows for my truck from a local junk yard. His kindness was suspicious and unfathomable: to offer such aid to me, the person who had sent the police to his apartment earlier that morning. Clearly someone was feeling a little guilty.

Without telling my boyfriend, I made preparations to hide out at my friend's. The friend with whom I was staying had been his rival in love, and once wanted my heart or at least a piece of it. The two of them fought like rabid dogs when the three of us were in a room together; my friend being the more vicious of the two, my boyfriend the more submissive. In college, I lived down the hall from this friend and sometimes I would go to his room and cry to him about my boyfriend. At the very least, he would hang out with me and play video games while he listened.

After one particularly bad fight with my boyfriend, I walked over to his dorm room crying. This time, he closed the door behind me, put his arms around me and ran his fingers through my long ebony hair. He looked uncomfortably deep into my eyes and slid his hand gently down my forearm. He secured it around my waist and pulled me close, slowly moving his lips towards mine.

"Hayley, just break up with him already and go out with me. I like you, I know you like me. We could be together," he came in for a kiss.

"Don't," I said and turned my head away. I was not a cheater and he had broken up with his girlfriend just the week before. Wouldn't we just be one another's rebounds?

When we first met, I would have gone out with him *if he was available,* but he was not. At that time, he had a girlfriend, but now that he *was* available, I was no longer free and too proud to dump my boyfriend for him because he had not dumped his girlfriend for me. For a while, I regretted this decision, but at the same time knew that he would not have been able to handle or understand what was going on inside my head. No one could.

I would not let my boyfriend find out where I would be hiding, though I wanted so badly to rub it in his face: the fact that I was staying with his biggest enemy, a guy who endlessly annoyed him when we were together in class and shamelessly flirted with me right in front of his face. I feared that if he discovered my location, my friend's car might be his next victim.

Finally, he got out of the shower and came back into the bedroom. I was so angry that I could not hold in my irritation and said what was on my mind about the windows and the girl. Screeching at him, we argued back and fourth while he scrambled to put on his clothes. I screamed. He did not yell as much as I did, rather, cowered out of fear or guilt. He denied everything, then became silent and crossed his arms before offering to pay for my replacement windows.

"Just give me the money now!" I demanded.

"I will if you fuckin' leave!" he yelled.

"Fine!" I screamed.

"How much are they? I have to go to the ATM."

"Three-hundred dollars!"

"I'll be right back," he said throwing on a jacket as he ran out the door. He was so obliging that I suddenly wished I had asked for more money.

I hastily shoved my clothes into a New England Patriots duffle bag, then surveyed the room to make sure I did not forget anything. *I could not wait to get out.*

I sat on his bed in silence and waited for him to come back with the money. There was a TV in the room, but I did not feel like watching it or even turning it on for background noise.

After a few hours passed and he had not returned, I became vengeful. On his desk sat a money order for $500, his monthly car payment. I held it in my hand and was about to rip it into pieces. I had done something similar to a boyfriend once before, but for some reason, I could not bring myself to do it this time. Maturity maybe? So instead, I folded it in half and hid it between two random books in his bookcase. He was not much of a reader. It would probably take him a few years to find it, *if he ever did.*

I waited all night for his return, well past midnight. Soon, I began to worry. Maybe he was not really going to give me the money. Or maybe he had changed his mind. Three-hundred dollars was a lot of dough and I had not even asked him for it. He offered. As the hours passed, I face-palmed myself for ending up in this situation to begin with.

The previous fall, I had broken up with him after he snuck off to the bar and returned in a drunken rage. When he returned, I naturally asked him where he had been. He was so wasted that he could not articulate an answer. He just mumbled and with one hand, awkwardly held out his cell phone and waved it around like he was trying to find reception.

At that moment, I noticed that typed across the phone's front display were the digits "911." Had he tried to call 911? Did something happen? Was there something wrong that I did not know about? I tried to take it from him to get a closer look. I was already terrified by his behavior. The discovery that someone had tried to call 911 from his phone for whatever reason freaked me out even more.

Calmly, I asked him if he was okay. He walked towards me grinning. I took a few steps backward then he swung his fist at my face.

I dodged it easily, but this time his violence did not go unnoticed. Neither of us realized that the residential advisor of my dorm had been standing behind us the entire time. The RA witnessed everything and reported the entire incident to Public Safety. As a result, my now ex-boyfriend was banned from the dorms permanently and only allowed on campus to attend his classes.

Tales of the night spread quickly across the small campus the same way a tsunami invades the land sweeping over houses and yards with ease. My college only consisted of two thousand students. That morning, when I walked out of my dorm to go to class, the students and staff stared at me as if I had a black eye. I pretended not to notice and walked by conveniently hiding my shame behind a pair of cheap sunglasses. They were silenced by my presence and did not resume their conversations until well after I passed by. I wondered what they thought of me.

Not a week went by before he contacted me again. I tried to ignore him, but he would not stop calling. It became so bad that I finally unplugged my phone from the wall and disconnected my cell phone so the ringing would stop. The second I plugged my phone back in, it started to ring incessantly again. He eventually wore me down and convinced me to go out to the parking lot to meet him.

"Sit with me in the car, it's freezing out here."

"I don't think that's a good idea," I said looking back at my dorm. It was either the car or the dorm. I could not stand out in the frigid weather all night. I got in the car.

Once in his car, he pressed his chapped lips against my smooth skin, and ran his hands down my back, trying to pry off sweater as he kissed me. "This is also probably a bad idea," I said again, as he slid my bra strap off of my left shoulder.

He continued to call and text me thereafter, but this time I was strong enough to ignore him. *Until Christmas Eve.* The holiday had created an unexpected longing in me. I texted him and we were instantly back on speaking terms. We met up, hooked up, and broke up, again.

I did not see him until some time in January, and it ended up being another huge mistake. I stayed at his place for several weeks as I unsuccessfully looked for jobs in the Burlington area. Jobs were not really what was on my mind.

What had brought me back to Vermont was the need for validation.

For weeks, I had been harboring disappointment over something I had done weeks earlier: cocaine. I feared judgment and did not tell anyone about it until I finally called him. I was expecting a negative reaction, and even more scrutiny. I felt relieved by his unfazed response. I was surprised that he did not hold my drug use against me. The fact that he liked me when I did not like myself was the only thing that made me feel better.

When it came to substances, I had been strong for so long, or at least *that's what I told myself*. Outwardly I put up a sturdy front, yet deep down inside I knew that my fortification could collapse at any moment; I was not strong, merely pretending. On this particular weekend, a longtime Irish friend happened to be *on holiday* in *The States*. We spent the night bar-hopping and as the evening wound down, we inevitably met up with my old boss for drinks. For me, the mood quickly changed from fun to fearful when I found myself in a car parked behind a shopping plaza snorting cocaine off a credit card.

"Can we get some coke?" My friend asked me.

"I dunno, can we?" I said looking at my ex-boss, whose reputation for having a cocaine penchant was longstanding.

"Let me make a phone call," she said while exiting the bar. Although she had recently completed a *program*, she had no qualms about it. I, however, began to reconsider.

At first, I tried to talk her out of it, "Are you sure you want to do this? Didn't you just get out of rehab?"

She merely rolled her eyes at me. "I just don't want to mess up your progress," I said.

"I still know my dealer's number by heart, so..."

"*So* what?" I asked.

"So, we've obviously been in touch." And that was it. Soon an old black man showed up at the bar. It was not at all suspicious until she and him disappeared into the cramped one person bathroom for what seemed like forever. Since it was so late and we were some of the last people dwindling at the bar, their absence was impossible not to notice.

As the night continued, I became agitated. We ran into a guy I knew from high school. In high school, he was blond and gorgeous with a irresistible smile and shocking blue eyes. Back then, lots of girls had wanted him including myself, but now he was frail and his once lucid eyes were punctuated with with deep dark circles likely resulting from years of drug use. When he figured out what we were doing, he wanted in. We attempted to avoid him and dodged out of the bar without saying goodbye.

My friend and I followed behind my ex-boss as she drove erratically across the city. Finally, she pulled into a shopping plaza, "What the fuck?"

She continued to drive through the lot until we were parked behind the building, shielded from the main road. My friend and I got out of the car and climbed into the back seat of hers. She sat in the driver's seat, the dealer in the passenger's seat.

For almost an hour, the dealer gave us excuses as to why he did not have any drugs on him. I became more and more paranoid as each minute passed, constantly looking out the window to ensure no one had noticed us parked behind the building. Eventually he pulled out a small baggie full of fine white powder. He had the drugs on him the entire time.

"You just wanted to be in the car with the cute Irish chick, didn't you?" My old boss accused him. I too had a feeling he had been holding out in order to optimize his time with my fair-haired foreign friend.

From where I sat, I watched the two of them snort lines off an American Express credit card passing it back and forth between them. Each time the lines disappeared, the dealer, unprompted, cut new ones and put the card back into circulation. I had no intention of joining in.

"I'm impressed by your willpower," my ex-boss said to me as she shoved a rolled-up dollar bill up her nose, "Hayley was always such a good girl," she said to her drug dealer. That's how they thought of me at work: the good girl, the sweet girl. They had no clue about the inner torment and tumultuous past I was hiding.

"I changed my mind," I said, surprising her.

"Hayley, you don't have to do it just because we are." I looked at her perplexed,

"Just hand me the card," I said as I put out my hand. I had done it before. Slowly the dealer scooped up a small amount of white powder with the corner of the credit card. I sniffed the miniscule mound of cocaine up one nostril and then he gave me another hit for the other.

In between lines, my boss and the dealer argued. He still had not sold her anything, rather he kept us at bay by sharing *his* supply with us. Now with cocaine in my bloodstream, I was even more anxious. Suddenly, my heart raced as headlights appeared from the side of the building.

Oh my God, we're going to get arrested. The car drove closer beaming its lights right onto us. My heart continued to pound until I realized that it was not a cop car, but a beat-up old Honda. The car pulled up next to mine and parked. As it pulled in, I saw the familiar face of the guy from the bar. His face was white as a ghost. His mid -80's era Honda was a sharp contrast to the expensive cars he drove in high school. He walked up to our window, trying to get in on the party.

Not a minute later, more headlights appeared from around the corner. *Now we were really going to get busted.* I braced myself and waited for the flashing lights of a cop car to appear at any second. The car stopped and turned off its engine. A girl got out of the car and walked up to ours. It was not a cop, but the coke fiend's extremely possessive girlfriend who had somehow followed him here. Now everyone in our car was annoyed. She joined her boyfriend at the driver's side window pleading for a hit.

"I'm getting out of here," I said to my Irish friend. "This is way too heated."

"Why?" She protested. "She didn't even buy the coke from him yet."

"So?"

"Well, we don't have to go so soon."

I waited a minute unsuccessfully debating in my mind whether or not she was right. *So soon?* It was almost 4 o'clock in the morning.

"I'm leaving," I said and opened the car door as the two standing outside scrambled to climb into my seat. My friend quickly snorted another line and followed reluctantly behind me. We got into my truck and pulled out from behind the store. I wondered how a cop had not noticed all the activity going on behind the building especially at this time of night. I pulled onto the street, and a car immediately pulled out behind me: this time it really was a cop car.

"Oh my God, there's a cop behind us!" Had they been there the entire time waiting for one of us to leave the plaza? Somehow I knew they had seen us drive out from behind the building, how couldn't they have?

"So what," my friend said non-nonchalantly. I balked at her lack of concern. From what she said, in her country, cocaine was illegal, but not entirely frowned upon or cracked down upon like it was here.

"So what? We could get arrested if they find out about the coke!"

"Really? In Ireland the cops don't really arrest you for *cocaine*." I looked at her like she was crazy.

"Well in this country, cocaine is a huge felony." I could not imagine how much trouble a foreigner would be in for breaking that kind of law while on vacation. I pictured the police detaining her and causing her to miss her flight back to the UK.

"We could go to jail!" Even if they did not nab me for the cocaine, I had been drinking all night. I had gotten a little carried away with the sour apple shots the bartender kept feeding us.

I looked into my rearview as I simultaneously tried to keep the car steady and my eyes on the road. It seemed like a lot of things to do at once, especially with the police creeping down my back. A picture of my disheveled mugshot flashed into my head, *nobody looks good at four in the morning.* The mug shot was not nearly as bad as the potential write-up in the local newspaper, "Elementary school teacher arrested for cocaine and drunk driving."

The police car was still behind me when we came to a red light at a major intersection. My mind frantically bounced between my options as I tried to decide which way to go: left or right? Which way would be the best choice to lose this tail? To the right was their jurisdiction and to the left was the city limits and consequently my home. The red light glowed as I pleaded with myself, *what should I do? Somebody please help!* Suddenly, a voice in my head urged me to, "Go Home!"

In retrospect, the choice had been obvious. I drew a deep breath and signaled left. Timidly, I hit the gas and started the long drive back to my house. I made my move, then held my breath and stared at the rearview mirror awaiting the police car to make theirs. To my sheer delight, the police turned right.

I brought my friend back to her uncle's house. As she exited the car, she muttered something about it "not even being pure cocaine. It was probably cut with ecstasy."

This made me even crazier than I already was. I knew all about ecstasy. I had seen a special about it on MTV; the drug was fierce and could put huge holes right through your brain. Tunnels! When I got home, I stayed up all night Googling the side effects and dangers of both drugs.

A few weeks passed, but I could not forgive myself for this moment of weakness. That's when I called my ex-boyfriend and told him about what happened. He was kind and assured me that I was not a horrible person. That night, I drove back to Vermont to see him.

One of the nights I was there, his bedroom was Arcticly cold. I begged him to raise the heat but he was too lazy to get out of bed. Sharp pangs pierced my lungs each time I inhaled the frigid air. Without realizing it, I soon became very ill.

With no health insurance, I put off going to the doctor. I struggled to get up and barely made it to work each day. Months before, I applied to several graduate school programs for an MFA in Creative Writing. It did not seem like I would be getting into any of these programs because each day, more rejection letters filled my mailbox. It appeared my decline in heath was directly proportional to my growing stack of bad-news-bearing papyrus.

I woke up one morning unable to move. With every breath, acute pain spread across my chest. For a few days now, I had called out of work so I could stay in bed. Although my ex-boyfriend and I had officially gotten back together during my last trip to Vermont, he had not called me in days. He could not even send me a quick text to see how I was feeling, let alone make a phone call. Sick and depressed, death was on my mind. With few friends in my hometown, a boyfriend, who was probably cheating on me, and no chance of getting into grad school, the future felt bleak.

Death became a welcome friend. For days, I stayed in bed untreated. Nobody knew how sick I was, not even me.

One morning, I contemplated whether or not I wanted to live anymore and came to the conclusion that I did not. I was not going to outright kill myself, but I was not about to go out of my way to try and save myself either. I was just going to go to sleep for a long time and let whatever happened happen. I started to doze off after making the conscious decision to lean towards death, but then my mother burst into my bedroom. Nervously, she began to recount to me what she just saw.

She was lying in her bed when she was suddenly awoken out of a deep sleep. She thought it was me that woke her, but when she opened her eyes, a figure wearing a black cloak stood in front of her staring quietly.

Now I was scared. What were the chances that at the exact same time I had been thinking of death, my mother got a visit from the Grim Reaper? He was obviously coming for me. Immediately, I asked her to drive me to the emergency room and $700 later, I was medicated and back in bed, where I would stay for the next four weeks.

During that month, my boyfriend did not visit me once. He did not send a card. He barely even called. I did not learn until months later that he used my absence as an opportunity to cheat on me *with that cheerleader and God knows who else.*

Despite this poor treatment, I clung to him like a lifeguard who had just saved me from drowning. Nothing was going right in my life and being with him was the only thing I could count on. But after he broke my windows and I found out he had cheated on me, I could no longer deceive myself.

It was not until long after midnight that he came back from wherever he had been.

"Do you have the money?" I asked.

"Here," he pulled three one-hundred-dollar bills out of his wallet and threw them at me like I was a cheap whore. I stuffed them into my pocket and slung my duffle bag over my shoulder. As I walked out of the room, I paused for a moment and leaned against the door frame,

"I'm leaving," I said, looking back at him.

"Bye," he said not even looking up from what he was doing to acknowledge me. A part of me secretly hoped that he would tell me not to go; that he would beg me to stay. I sighed to myself. Once in the foyer, I stared at the door for a moment before I brought myself to open it. Outside it was classically raining. It had been raining all afternoon, and earlier, with the help of duct tape, I bandaged each window frame with black garbage bags.

Now outside, I pulled the bags off my truck one at a time and shook off the rain drops. I threw them onto the passenger's seat then climbed in. It was a cool night, but bearable. I looked behind me to see if he had come outside to try and stop me from leaving. *Nope.* There was no sign of him.

I pulled my truck towards the end of his driveway and hit the brake. I looked in my rearview mirror. I could see him in the picture window with his back turned away. He was having a conversation with his roommate. I waited a few seconds, but he did not as much as look out of the window. He did not try to stop me. I took my foot off the brake and drove away.

It was dark and still raining when I arrived at my friend's house. Before I arrived, he told me he would be sleeping, but said he would leave the door unlocked for me. I crept into the dark house and followed his instructions settling into one of the spare rooms, he had left blankets and towels on the desk for me. He left for work early that morning and it was not until late evening that I saw him.

My now ex-boyfriend began texting my phone every five minutes. Though I wanted to think that it was because he still had feelings for me, I knew it was because he was wondering where I was. He knew my windows had not come in yet, that they would not come in for several more days, and that I would not drive back to Connecticut without them. He tried to guess where I was, and even guessed correctly, but I would not give up my location. That night, before my friend got home from work, my now ex-boyfriend had talked me into going back to his apartment. I packed my things and put on my jacket, greeted my friend as he walked in the kitchen door.

"Where are you going?" he asked.

"Back to, well, you know..."

"Are you kidding me?"

"No."

"For over a year I have heard you bitch about him countless times. I even left the door unlocked for you in the middle of the night so you could stay with me *at my parent's house* to get away from him because *he smashed your windows.* And now you are just going to waste my time and go back to him?"

He was pissed. He hung his jacket on the hook and placed his keys on the counter. He kept his eyes on me as he walked over to the door and dead bolted the lock. "You are not going back to him."

I met my ex at Nectars, the popular Burlington bar credited with discovering the band Phish. I noticed his slight build as he peered at me from the corner of the room. His sandy blond hair and blue eyes made him stand out, but his chiseled features told me he was probably the type of guy I should stay away from.

That night at the bar, I sat at a table surrounded by beautiful friends: one busty Brazilian who blatantly bounced up and down to attract all kinds of attention, and another slight blond Barbie type --- the type I wished I was, but wasn't. Despite their high levels of attractiveness and sex appeal, they faded out of his focus as he narrowed his eyes in at me. He walked by the table and uttered a quick "Hello."

"Hi," I replied, apprehensively.

He disappeared as quickly as he had arrived. The band got back on stage and resumed their set. I looked up and was surprised to see that he was up there with the band behind the keyboard. *Oh great, a musician.* This was just another strike against him.

Eventually we got up to leave and go to another bar. As my friends and I walked out the door, he rushed over to me to get my number. He suggested that we meet up for a drink. I gave him my digits, but I never heard from him.

The following semester, I ran into him in my Shakespearian theater and literature course. Coincidentally, he was trying to finish his degree at the same school I attended.

When it was time to put in requests for scenes, I suggested that we work together. We both thought it would be fun and requested the balcony scene from *Romeo and Juliet.* Though we requested *Romeo and Juliet,* our instructor assigned us to the nunnery scene from *Hamlet.* He was Hamlet and I, Ophelia. One afternoon, he invited me up to his apartment to *study our lines.* Instead we got sidetracked by his electric piano.

The large keyboard dominated the space of his tiny living room.

"Can you sing?" he asked sitting down at the bench.

"Um..." I replied, "Not really."

"Are you sure?" he asked. "We need a female vocalist for our band." I thought about it.

"I think I'm going to have to practice a little and sing for you some other time." I was too shy to sing for him, or anybody really. I had not yet found my voice.

"That's cool. Can you play?"

"A little," I said.

He motioned for me to sit down on the bench beside him and laughed nervously as my leg brushed against his. His hands trembled as I got closer.

He played the opening bar from Coldplay's "Trouble." I was impressed. "You can play Coldplay?"

He smiled at me then continued to own the piano blowing through a repertoire of Supertramp, The Doors, and Coldplay.

"Could you teach me to play 'Trouble?'" I always wanted to learn some Coldplay.

We began with the 17-note opening. Then he took my hand and encouraged me to follow along with his. Clumsily, I hit the keys. He just sat there smirking.

"Not bad." He continued to shake nervously every time his hand brushed mine.

I never went back. Instead I crashed at my friend's place until the windows finally arrived. I waited at the mechanics while they installed the new windows. It only took them about five minutes to replace the passenger side window. I would be out of Vermont sooner than I thought. Finally, things seemed to be turning around for me. I smiled at the mechanic, happy that things were going so smoothly, but rather than smile in return, he diverted his glance.

Soon my mechanic walked over to me, "The glass place sent the wrong winder for the driver's side," he had some kind of accent.

"How long will it take to get another one?"

"They don't have this particular winder at their shop, so it could be days, possibly weeks, before we kin find a replacement."

I had made it through hell and landed in purgatory. So badly, I wanted to leave Vermont.

"Just mail it to me."

Every time his hands flew across the keyboard I felt dwarfed by his talent. In awe. I listened as he jumped from pop music songs to classical sonatas. *All from memory.* I loved hearing him play the various preludes and symphonies whose names I could never remember. Only one of the songs stuck permanently in my mind: Chopin's "Nocturne Opus 9 Number 2."

From the first time he played it, I became paralyzed by the beauty of its melody. As I listened, the various notes and climaxes shifted from musical vibrations to a story about two lovers.

It was summertime, very long ago, during an era where women only wore dresses and men wore boisterous white wigs. On most days, a young woman sat under a willow tree working on her needlepoint undisturbed, until one particular day she looked up from her craft and accidentally caught the gaze of a young gentleman. He coyly tried to walk past, but could not avert his eyes.

Each day he created a new excuse to stroll past the willow. No matter how hard he tried, he could not will himself to look away. As time passes, she begins to await his presence. Frequently looking up from her embroidery, she counts every grueling minute.

They are not lovers at first. Soon, the dance of temptation commences; should they or shouldn't they, the confusion, the indecision, and then heartbreak. They become intertwined, but then they unravel, only to tumble into one another's arms again and again.

After listening to the nocturne many times closely, it was certain that in the end they could never be together; the moon was the only witness to their love's demise. But on moonlit nights, she still tiptoes through the evening and hides behind the weeping willow to wait for him to pass so they can once again begin their tragic lovers' dance.

In addition to Chopin, he played the entire Coldplay tracks with ease. I felt like a child in comparison, trying to thump out those first 17 notes of "Trouble." I had taken piano lessons for two years in middle school. Back then, I was much less attentive to my gay balding piano teacher than with my attractive and talented classmate.

I was not interested in him as much as I was seduced by his music. He was the Pied Piper and I was a lowly rat who clung to him for life even as the relationship became progressively worse and abusive. I remember the first time I tried to leave him. It happened in the midst of an icy storm.

"You never loved me, Hayl."

"You're drunk!"

"Because if you love me, you wouldn't walk out me like this."

"What?" I scoffed. "That's not true! I do love you, and if you loved me, you wouldn't drink so much. You'd get help! You'd take care of yourself so we could be together!"

I turned away from him and walked towards the door.

"No Hayl, no, that's asking me to change. If you love someone you don't ask them to change, I never tried to change you!"

"Change me? Why would I need to change? I never hurt you! You're the one who hurts me and everyone around you *when you drink*!"

"Oh come on, Hayl. You're such a baby. Just because I get a little mean when I'm drunk, doesn't mean I have a problem. I always do *that*, I always treat my friends like shit when I drink, it's fun!"

"Fun? It's *fun* to hurt people who care about you?"

"Whatever Hayl, you just don't get it. Fuck you!"

Each curse was an arrow to my heart; a heart that broke a little more each time he swore at me. I slammed the door behind me just as he shouted, "If you want to be with me, you need to accept me for me!"

"No thanks!" I yelled back through the solid oak. I stomped down the hallway and out into the bitter night. So quiet and rigid, alone, I walked up and down Burlington's cobblestone streets. They were handsomely lit by ornate street lanterns and canopied by strands of white Christmas lights strung from one shop's rooftop to the next. On a blustery night like this, just squinting at them gave them the appearance of nearby constellations like Perseus and Cetus.

I passed a few of the bars we were invited to play at before his behavior got us both kicked out of the band. My stomach hurt at the thought of those memories, *now so painful*. He claimed to love me, yet only thought of himself. It was more important that he maintain his *musician's lifestyle* than our relationship.

As a gifted pianist, he felt entitled to the destructive path of the drugs, sex, and rock 'n roll. In fact, he acted as if this was his birthright. He was doomed to be just another artist who wasted his talent in the pursuit of some sort of psychological oblivion.

That night as I trudged through the snow, all I could think about was giving him another chance.

Then my phone vibrated. He had finally texted me, "I love you babe. Isn't love enough?"

Love? Enough? Didn't Sonny and Cher write a song based on that premise? Even *they* got divorced.

"Not always," I texted back.

During my last winter semester, when I walked through the campus at night alone, I could feel him slipping away from me. Snowflakes silently wafted to the ground and reminded me of the Valentines' Day blizzard, the weekend he became more than just another guy to me.

Until then, he had only been a dingy old beach oyster, very easy to overlook. It was not until the second or third glance that I realized the oyster might reveal a pearl. We had no other choice but to spend the entire weekend in bed because the severe weather buried our cars beneath five feet of Vermont snow.

I sat in the makeshift lobby and watched the mechanic and the glass guy stick a large sheet of clear plastic over my windowless frame. Then I got into the car and drove away. Halfway through my drive home it began to drizzle. Within minutes, the plastic window began to slowly curl backwards. Then it made a loud noise as it flew off on one side flapping in the wind like an injured gull.

I pulled over at the next gas station to stick the plastic back on, but it would not adhere to the truck's dewey metal. In frustration, I ripped the whole thing off and threw it in the back seat. Rain intermittently hit me in the face as I drove. It did not matter that I drove windowless. All that mattered was that I drove home.

About a week later, my window arrived in a large cardboard box. Installing it ended up being a much easier job than expected. My father and I had no problem putting the window into the door frame, it was not until we rolled it up that we realized that the glass did not fit. I called my friend's husband who was a glass man in Connecticut. He pulled out his book and asked me to read him the window's serial number. I read it to him. He immediately asked me to read it again, then informed me that it was not the right window for the make or model of my vehicle.

Once again, they had sent me the wrong window. I could not believe it. At this point, I felt like God was trying to drive this point home. For the next two weeks, I drove around town humiliated with a barely clinging plastic "window" stuck to my ride, until I finally got the phone call I was waiting for. My new window was ready. The only problem was I had to drive three hours to Southern Vermont to get it.

The ride through Western Mass and into Southern Vermont was painful. Though I was still over two hours away from my old home in Northern Vermont, I was driving the same exact route I took to get there.

Now my windows were intact, but my life was another story. I had few friends back in Connecticut after I distanced myself from my *friends* who did drugs and partied. I no longer had an interest in going to bars.

After the lengths my now ex-boyfriend went through to get rid of me, I was stunned when he started to call. I had no problem ignoring him, but once again the calls did not stop. Both the calls and texts were endless. This time I blocked his number, but soon handwritten love letters started to arrive in my mailbox. How odd it was to profess his love for me after the relationship was beaten beyond repair; if only he bothered to do this while we were still together. His final phone call was answered by my very angry mother.

I was back in my parent's house. My windows were fine, but my heart was in pieces. My faith in love crumbled. I knew people who had been in love and heard stories about those lucky ones, yet somehow, love had always alluded me.

At the time, the concept of a true love as something real and reciprocated paralleled my feelings about God and faith; sometimes it felt attainable, but most of the time it felt like it was reserved for everyone but me. I reminded myself that I was lucky that they only went after my windows. I shivered at the thought of a worse scenario —— a potential Nancy Kerrigan-style attack. From this perspective, I felt fortunate.

It was difficult for me to accept that someone I considered, at the very least a friend, could be so merciless. It saddened me that after spending so much time with this person, that we would never speak again.

Each night my heart ached unrelentingly over his betrayal, and the sadness and desolation I felt after moving back to my hometown and away from my friends. Amplified by the lack of true love in my life made my suffering almost unbearable.

One morning, I unexpectedly awoke from a beautiful dream. I was on a cruise ship, it was early in the morning, the sun had just started to come up. I went outside onto the main deck. I walked to one side of the ship. I leaned against the rail and watched the pastel hues of pinks, blues, and oranges, dance gloriously on the ocean's soft currents. It was not often I got up to see an early morning sunrise and certainly had never seen one this beautiful. Upon a second glance at the water, I was stunned by what I saw. Within the glittering ocean waded thousands of beautiful dolphins.

II

Andromeda

There will be time enough for tears; this hour is all we have for rescue-

We spent the summer at his family's beach house on the Rhode Island shore. Somehow we ended up there almost every weekend baking lazily in the sun. It was a beautiful setting for the beginning stages of any relationship and we were just getting to know each other. That summer, like two children frolicking in the sand, we carried a plastic pail as we traversed the beach looking for stones.

The beach stones in Rhode Island were unlike anything I ever saw. Not in Florida, the Connecticut coast, or anywhere in between had I seen such beautiful stones and the Rhode Island beaches were bountiful with every size and color. Soft to the touch, these oval jewels looked like small candies. Each and every one, more perfect than the last; their uniformity took on a manufactured feel. I fell in love with them instantaneously.

I thought back to the beach stones from my home state, Connecticut, which were more like rocks than anything. The Connecticut coast did not really have many stones worth mentioning. One time, however, I found a perfect piece of quartz the size and shape of a large egg. I was five-years-old. It was early winter, and I begged my parents to take me to the beach. I barely noticed the frigid air as I sat on my beach blanket chomping on a peanut butter and fluff sandwich. Ignoring the cold breeze, and despite my parent's protests I attempted to go for a swim. Where the water met the sand is where I found the rock. At first I thought it was an egg. I lifted it out of the sand and examined it.

"Don't you think that maybe it could be an egg, Daddy?" I wanted to believe that it was an egg.

He said that he did not think so, but after asking him the same question several times, he finally said, "I don't know, *maybe*," to placate my child's mind.

The whole ride home, I smiled as I held it in my hands caressing its smooth shell. Over and over again, I told myself that it was not a rock, but an egg. Even then, deep down inside, I knew the truth.

I met him at a party and there was an instant attraction. At first, it seemed that maybe he was the one guy who was everything the others were not. He was nice, polite, and gentlemanly. He loved children and animals or at least, that's what he told me.

On our first date, although he said and did all the right things, somewhere in the back of my mind, I got an inkling that perhaps he was just acting. Trying to dissect and understand the root of my suspicion sent me into a mental frenzy; this idea that his persona was false and somewhere behind his dull blue eyes harbored a psychopath. Even though he looked and acted like a decent man, something was missing; he was like a well-preserved shell in someone's ocean-themed bathroom, extrinsically beautiful, yet dead inside.

Like a bad actor assigned to the role of nice guy, he went through the motions without any emotions behind them. My family and friends liked him. I confided to a few, my fear that perhaps he was just pretending to be nice and in reality was truly insane.

They laughed at me. My reputation for being overly-cautious preceded everything I said. They took it upon themselves to explain to me what my problem was: after being in so many bad relationships I was scared because a nice guy was interested in me, for once. Regardless of what they told me, I still thought that I might be right. At the time, I was not strong enough to break the dangerous cycle of not listening to my inner voice. Of course, I wanted to believe my friends and family. What was the alternative? Throwing myself back into the dating pool and trying again? I wanted to believe that I was wrong *though everything in me screamed that I was right.* Who does not want a nice guy to look out for them? To come home to every night? To (insert other ridiculously overused love cliche here)? All of this is what he literally promised me during our first official date. He also promised that if I went out with him that he would never leave me and I believed him.

During my entire life, love was the one thing I wanted more than anything else. I wanted to hold it, to possess it, to swim in it; I wanted it to be mine once and for all. Since I was a little girl, it was all I dreamed about. I wanted to soak it up and bathe in it like a girl who spends her entire day on the beach trying to get a tan. What I truly wanted was the same thing that everyone else wanted and here he was literally handing it over to me, no strings attached, and promising to be my knight in shining armor, too.

At the beginning of the Rhode Island summer, I only picked up the white stones, but not all the white stones. They had to be the purest of quartz. I could not tolerate a single flaw, and threw any white ones with dark veins back into the water, no matter how beautiful.

After a few more trips to Rhode Island, the black stones began to catch my eye. When damp, they looked like onyx. As time passed, I became more flexible with my stone selections; I now collected not only the whitest of white, but also the blackest of black stones. Only the purest of each color would do, but then I began to see potential in the gray ones as well. I visualized how beautiful the larger stones would look in my garden. So I began picking up those as well.

Eventually, I saw the beauty in the other stones which varied in hues of gray and tan and red and orange. Some of the gray stones even looked blue.

When I met him, I was very vulnerable because the weekend before our meeting, I had been dumped by someone else. After confiding to that guy that years earlier I had been raped, he suddenly ended all contact with me. In my whole life, I never felt like a bigger piece of trash. It was horrific, the way he immediately discarded me over something that was out of my control. So when the new guy actually showed up on our date, I was so elated that he actually showed up that I did not even think about stopping to closely examine his character. Because of what happened the week prior, I did not think anyone would ever want me again.

The morning of our first date, my first article about life after rape was published. He knew I had an article coming out and I knew he planned to read it. He just did not know what it was about. I nervously walked into the bar that evening fearing that he would not show up; that he would run away from me, too.

Over the next few months, I thought it was peculiar that he never got angry over anything. Sometimes I would ask him, "How is it that you are so calm all the time? Are you secretly hiding some kind of explosive temper?"

"No," he would say, "I never get angry."

Still, something about his demeanor deceived this claim; *that he never got mad.* So many of his mannerisms reminded me of a friend's old boyfriend. Not only was this man spiteful and verbally abusive to her, but he also spoke shockingly disrespectful to me and our other friends when we visited. That man concealed an atrocious temper. It was difficult to ignore how closely my boyfriend's attitude and mannerisms aligned with his. I shrugged it off and tried to convince myself that it was just coincidental.

As the summer dwindled, we began to grow apart. Around my birthday, we took a trip to Florida. I think he thought it might bring us back together, this beautiful vacation. It did not change a thing about our relationship, in fact, it only strained it more.

On the way home, he got violently angry at me and screamed in my face, spraying spit as he shouted. Somewhere around South Carolina, he dumped me. I was stunned. I could not stop sobbing, and there was at least 16 more hours of driving ahead of us. I rested my head on the passenger side window and cried into my sleeve trying to ignore him as he continuously swore and screamed "Stop crying!"

"Just stop," I choked out, "just leave me alone; you're hurting me."

"You can cry all you want," he stated emotionless. "I won't feel sorry for you. I *don't* feel sorry for you. You caused *this*. *This* is all your fault."

He kept raging, kept yelling, and kept screaming even as I began to hyperventilate. That night, he called me a cunt. He was angry because once again, he overdrew his bank account. Prior to our trip, he did this frequently without my help. This time he put the blame on me, not because he spent all this money on me (I paid my own way), but because the trip was my idea.

During the winter, we grew farther apart. The cold and blustery weather mimicked our relationship. He often called me names and ridiculed me for not working, even though I never asked him for money and had enough of my own to stay afloat. The thing is *I was working*, it just was not work that he considered work. I was trying to finish writing a book.

The only way I was able to stay with him was by suppressing my instinct to leave; I was drunk through a good part of our relationship. My behavior, though common, was less than normal. I still had not come to terms with the fact that this complete head case was indeed the same guy I had met months earlier.

Throughout my life, my family called me overly sensitive and now he did, too. I started to think that perhaps he was not treating me bad. That perhaps I was just being *too sensitive.* He quickly agreed with this idea, that he was not mean and it was just that I was too sensitive. Still, it was as if my eyes deceived me. He opened the car door and was always very courteous to me in public. Was he abusive? Or was I too sensitive?

My feelings for him ebbed and flowed with his displays of anger. At high tide, when his anger seethed, my emotions retreated inland towards higher ground to avoid drowning. When the tide went out again, I would peer over the bluff and when it was clear, slowly creep back down to the shore.

Thing got progressively worse. I felt like I was trapped on an island in the middle of a hurricane. I grew to need him more and more, and somehow, the more I needed him, the more he resented me. Screaming, swearing, and all kinds of abuse ensued. Sometimes he drove fast just to scare me. He was cruel. Nothing was sacred when it came to tormenting me; he sped through a windy mountain pass where my friend had been killed years earlier in an automobile accident caused by speeding.

I begged him to slow down. He laughed and drove faster. The more I begged, the angrier he got. As he bobbed and weaved around the cliff and teetered close to the edge, I begged him for my life. He grinned maniacally deriving pleasure from my fear. He turned his head towards me and screamed "Shut the fuck up," as loud as he could into my ear.

I grasped my ear in pain. At such close range, his voice pierced deep into the canal and inevitably left the hearing in my left ear permanently damaged.

As time passed, I became so drained that I could no longer concentrate on writing my book. To clear my mind, I took weekly trips to the shore to collect sea glass. It was something I liked doing as a child with my aunt. I cried as I walked up and down the beach alone. At first, I mourned the feeling of worthlessness he had engrained in me because of my employment status, but soon my focus became lost in the sand in my quest for mermaid tears.

Mermaid tears was a more whimsical name for sea glass. In general, there was something romantic about the glass. A very worn down piece could have been ruminating in the ocean for decades. Though I had no scientific way of dating the glass, my imagination ran away to another time and place picturing the origin of each piece I unearthed from the sand. Many of the weathered shards had obvious sources, but still there was no way of knowing how they ended up on each particular shore. Perhaps, some of the pieces originated from bottles that once carried messages to distant lovers; messages that were never received.

It is more likely that the glass originated from bottles left by local fisherman after sharing a few beers. I used to think that sea glass traveled from shore to shore. I imagined that the geographic origin of the glass was as ambiguous as the rest of its story and that perhaps, the glass even originated from far-off continents.

I was wrong. It turns out that the beaches with the best glass were once dumps where people left trash and bottles. This implied that the glass stayed forever on its beach of origin to be continuously tossed and thrown by the sea for many years until it was recovered.

At first, he went with me and we collected the glass together, but after our first excursion, I was on a sea glass kick. A few days later, I went back down to the shore in the middle of the week while he was working. He asked me not to go down and insisted that I wait until the weekend so he could go with me. However, when the weekend came, he no longer had any interest in going. I was glad I did not wait for him and went alone anyways.

I spent hours walking around the beach with my head turned downwards towards the sand. It was a brisk day and I couldn't believe how quickly the time went by. When I got home, I located all the sea glass I'd collected over the years and threw it together with my new pieces. I spent the rest of the night separating the pieces by color and placing them into various Mason jars.

I had a large jar for the clear white glass and a small jar for the opaque. I had a large jar of green glass and a small jar of lime green. I had another small jar with only a few pieces of blue tinted opaque glass, which I figured must have been a rare color due to its scarcity.

I had another large jar filled with root beer colored glass and a small jar with honey brown pieces. My favorite pieces were the ones that had letters and designs imprinted on them. I had one with a cursive letter "S" and another with a sunburst pattern. Sorting the glass by color was extremely meditative, and I found myself wanting to continue even after the task was completed. I schemed about when I would take my next trip to the beach.

Spontaneously, I went to the shore again the following day. This really pissed him off. I even set my alarm clock so I didn't waste precious glass-collecting time sleeping. That morning, I awoke to an icy drizzle, so I hit the snooze button. What more could I expect collecting sea glass in the middle of February?

By afternoon, the rain seemed to slow. The news channel warned of thunderstorms, but I longed to go back. Abruptly I jumped out of bed and decided to take my chances.

For a long time I wanted to move to the beach, Florida, Hawaii, somewhere warmer than New England. While at the same time, I'd been taking my one hour drive from the Connecticut shore for granted.

After several hours of collecting the glass, the sun began to set leaving me no choice but to return home. Once home, I took my jars of sorted glass off the shelf and poured them onto my rug with the day's newest acquisitions.

Sorting it over again, I obsessed over the color organization, noticing that there were many more variations of green glass than I had jars. Aside from the lime green, which had its own jar, and the blue opaque, which also had its own jar, other variants of greens began to stand out. There was dark green, medium green, light green, and light opaque green.

It racked my brain as to how I would store them because I did not have enough jars! I supposed that the dark and medium greens could easily be combined, while the two variants of lighter colored greens could be stored together. Or maybe, I could buy more jars.

I still could not decide whether I should separate them into four distinct jars or two jars with the colors combined. And what if I did separate the greens? Would I then have to go back and pick through the browns and whites, too? I decided not to separate every color variant. Rather, I stuck to outliers and separated the lime greens, opaque blues, and lilacs from the bulk.

Sitting on the floor, I realized that obsessing over the separation and categorization of sea glass by color grade was equivalent to the ramblings of a mental patient, and if someone who didn't know better walked by me as I sat on the floor of my bedroom arranging and rearranging those smooth glass shards over and over again, they could have easily mistaken me for one. While in actuality, these were the thoughts of a person who'd been beaten down for so long that they just did not know what to do with themselves anymore. Someone who was just trying to create and maintain some sense of structure in a life that was otherwise falling apart.

Later that night, I proudly texted him an image of the sea glass. It looked beautiful on the shelf, arranged by color in their respective mason jars. The picture depicted my collection in all its glory: jars of dark green, light green, lime green, opaque blue, opaque, white, brown, and honey brown sea glass.

Seeing my collection motivated him to search for glass with me once again. Since he was always short on cash, collecting sea glass together was the perfect date. Not only was it something we could do together, but it was something we could do for free. Soon he found reasons to stop taking me to the beach to collect glass. Then he stopped taking me to his family's beach house for the weekend. He blamed it on the cost of gas and anything else he could think of.

In between looking for writing jobs, I continued to visit the beach. In addition to the angst he created in me over the fact that I still did not have a job, my own frustration increased as my job search waned on.

He went with me to the beach a few more times, but turned everything into a competition in which he was always the gloating champion. Who would find the most glass? He would. Who would find the rarest colors? He did.

At first I thought he was joking, *competing against me.* I never liked competition. I always rendered comparing yourself to others useless. His competition against me did not end there. One day he announced that his cooking was better than mine. I did not care whose was better, but I did care that his discretion with words was comparable to an man who carries a loaded gun without a safety.

By early spring I was certain there would be no new additions to my rock collection. As I sorted through them, I happened upon a teeny tiny perfectly round piece of sea glass. Though the Rhode Island beaches had plentiful amounts of beach stones, it was rare to find sea glass. A few times, we looked for it but had little luck. Glass was sparse and we found only a few tiny pieces. One day he found a minute piece of root beer glass that the ocean had shaped into a perfect circle.

Since he did not have a bag and I did, he asked me to hold onto it for him. *Sure,* I thought. *I'll hold onto it for you.* I really liked the piece. I wondered if he knew that when I added it to my bag of rocks that he would never see it again.

"I'll give it to you when we get back to the beach house," I lied. *Please God, forgive me*, it was perfect, so round, and so smooth.

Dejectedly, I sorted through the stones. After gathering them together, I divided them into rows of four by color variations and hues, just like I had with the sea glass. My boyfriend became increasingly distant. He now adamantly refused to take me to the beach house and made it very clear he would not be taking me anywhere to collect sea glass. In the end, I did get him to take me to the beach house one last time, but he really made me pay for it.

Whenever he did something that I wanted to do, he would verbally assault me afterwards. And even after he reamed me a new one, he made it a point to acknowledge that once again, I was the one who always got my way. The concept itself was crazy and I could not make sense of it. If I always got my way why was I so unhappy?

You see, the truth is I was poor and he was cheap. Though he made decent money, he only worked enough hours to pay a minimal amount of his bills. I felt that collecting beach treasures was an inexpensive but rewarding activity, something a guy like him would view as the ultimate cheap date. The location of the beach alone was breathtaking no matter what time of the day it was and more importantly, it did not cost any money!

His disinterest in pleasing me grew proportionately to the length of our relationship. I should have known from the beginning that the relationship was a sham. I was so convinced that his feelings for me were true that I never stopped to think about my feelings for him, *which were nonexistent*. Often he confessed that he loved me profusely and accused me of not loving him back. He was right, I did not, though at the time I tried to convince myself otherwise. There were so many things that I ignored, so many things that should have alerted me that he was lying.

For one, I should have known by the way he hated everything about me that he did not love me. *Everything.* Every activity I suggested, restaurant, or movie I picked out, no matter how critically or locally acclaimed it was he hated it, yet basked in the wonder of any activity he chose for us to partake. It hurt my feelings. Especially the time I spent several hundred dollars on a trip to Burlington.

Burlington, Vermont was the place where I had spent the last of my college years scampering from bar to bar in between break ups, and dining at some of the best eateries all while taking in the scenery. Every time I drove through the mountains of Vermont and emerged at the glorious shores of Lake Champlain, surrounded by the Adirondack Mountains, I felt at home again. Though it was the graveyard where my previous relationship was laid to rest, Burlington would always have my heart.

On our drive home from this wonderful weekend where I took him to some of the best and most expensive restaurants in the city, he told me that he hated Vermont and was completely unimpressed by Burlington. His words were an emotional slap in the face.

It was not only that. I should have known by the way he fucked me that he did not love me. I cringe to think of sex with him, he was so beastly and disheveled, and *not the good kind of beastly either.* The way he thrusted into me like he had not had sex in a decade *every time* was tiresome. With little eye contact and a lot of physical aggression he treated me more like a blow-up doll than a

46

person. Never once did we make love, although it was not always completely violent and fast. Sometimes he would slow down and go gentle, but he would not sustain this desired pace for long. Most nights I just wanted to put my clothes back on and go home. Cuddling with him was even worse and I hated sleeping over.

I was desperate and lonely at the time. However, this was not the first relationship where upon waking in the morning, I was so jolted by who lay next to me that my immediate reflex was to run out of their house and never come back. With my previous boyfriend, I often awoke wanting to kick him out of my bed and sometimes did, quickly slamming and locking the door behind him. I pretended I did not feel this way. And with this one I was drunk the first six months of our relationship and every weekend afterwards.

I was so lost that when he professed to love me, I could not help but hang on the hope that it was true. On our last trip to Rhode Island, his physically violent side began to surface. In the past, he screamed in my face, screamed over me, screamed so loud that every molecule in my body responded with tension and fear. Shouting into my face, he backed me up against a wall of frames holding photographs of his family. He did not stop screaming even as the pictures began to slip off their nails one by one and crash onto the floor.

When I think about how I allowed him to treat me, I become a sad grieving woman; an attendee at my own funeral, remorseful and unable to change what led to my demise. Now, I could not believe I let him talk to me in this way, but then I remember how pathetic and brainwashed I was at the time. The last time we went to the house in Rhode Island, we had stayed over for convenience. That night, we visited a friend in New London. After hanging out, we were tired and much closer to the beach house than our homes near Waterbury. The following morning was beautiful and sunny.

For months leading up to that day, I had been dying to expand my sea glass collection, but every time I asked him to go with me, he angrily refused to accompany me to the beach. Most weekends he complained that he did not have the money to take me out. *So why not go to the beach* I wondered, where the only expenditure was the gas it took to get there? Always, he refused to go, and most recently he came up with a new excuse as to why he did not want to. When he first refused to go he warned me never to ask him again. Unprompted, he followed up with a newer and wussier excuse, "I don't want to go because it hurts my neck to look down for the glass."

"Then don't look," I said, "just take me because I want to go. *You know I'm afraid to go alone.* You could just sit on the bench while I look for glass."

He knew how traumatized I was from my life, from being raped, and in the beginning he was sympathetic or at least feigned that he was. Now he used my fears against me. He would not let me crutch on him anymore; he refused to even let me lean on him, though he was the one who crippled me and made me dependent on him in the first place. He knew that I would never go to Bridgeport alone. Though the city held one of my favorite sea glass collecting locations, it also had one of the highest crime rates in the state. Knowing that I could not bring myself to go alone; he withheld his company and support, and instead helped me to construct a self-imposed prison.

"It hurts my neck too much," he whined, "and I know if I go with you, even just to *accompany you,* as you claim, so you can find glass, that I will end up looking for glass anyways instead of sitting on the bench like you've suggested."

Apparently the act of collecting sea glass was too painful for this 250-pound construction worker to bear.

Here we were at his family's ocean front property. One step off the porch and your feet hit sand. We were literally on the beach and he still refused to collect glass with me. He would not even sit out on the patio with me in the sun. It was the first warm day of the year, as our spring consisted mainly of rain and chilly temperatures. Not only did he not want to sit on the beach, but he wanted to go back to his sister's house in Connecticut and just sit around and watch TV with her family.

It did not make sense. Perhaps he was cheating on me? Or perhaps the only reason he did not want to stay on the beach with me was because *I* so badly wanted to stay to enjoy the beautiful weather. Maybe he just wanted to make me suffer.

It quickly turned into an argument. I left the house and sat outside to cool off. He followed me and hounded me incessantly trying to prolong the fight.

"Please stop," I said calmly. "I am done fighting with you."

He persisted. I stood up and walked back into the house, went into one of the first floor bedrooms, and closed the door behind me. He followed me.

"Leave me alone," I said. "I need space."

He grimaced, shut the door, and plopped himself down in front of it. My eyes widened.

"Let me out!" I demanded.

With a smile on his face, he silently shook his head 'no.' Terrified, I began to cry.

He moved out of my way. I opened the door and ran into the living room, but even then, he followed close behind me like a shadow. I sat down on the couch and he stood directly in front of me, inching closer and closer to me until his legs were locked against my knees. He looked down at me and grinned as if he was saying, "What are you gonna do about it now?"

Because he positioned himself so close to me, there was no way I could stand up. I was scared.

"Stop it!" I screamed, "Stop!"

Somehow he snapped out of it. We stayed a few more hours. I sat outside in the sun while he stayed inside with the blinds drawn shut watching TV like an old man. He did eventually go to the beach with me.

As we walked the length of the beach, I thought about our relationship. Recently, my aunt pointed out to me that I changed since I started going out with him. She said that parts of my identity were missing and wanted to know why I never got dressed up or wore make-up anymore.

For one thing, he never got dressed up to go out with me anywhere. In fact, he might have picked his clothes up off the floor for all I knew. He had even shown up at my house wearing holey shirts and sneakers.

After the first few times he picked me up dressed so incredibly down, I began to feel uncomfortable because I was so dressed up. I always wore beautiful scarves and jewelry, bright colors, with make-up to match. In time, I began to resent the fact that he did not try one bit to impress me, let alone bother to iron his clothes. So I began dressing casually, jeans, t-shirt, and little jewelry, if any.

"This isn't the Hayley I know," she said. "For the last six months, you have been dressing like a slob... like you just rolled out of bed. You don't even comb your hair."

I disagreed with her and explained why I had little desire to look good for someone who could care less about looking good for me.

"Just tell me one thing," she said, "Why don't you wear make-up anymore?"

Every time I wore make-up, instead of telling me that I looked pretty, he would say, "You don't need make-up, you're naturally beautiful."

Though I found this flattering, I responded by saying, "Thanks, but I look even better with make-up. *Everyone does.*"

Then he would counter, "I like you without make-up better."

I usually did not respond and just rolled my eyes.

After recounting this to my aunt, she insinuated that the whole thing was a ploy, "That's bullshit. Naturally beautiful? He was trying to *ugly* you up, to make you blend in."

A riptide had pulled me out to the sea. Walls of water began to cave in around me as she slowly adjusted my perception. The entire time I failed to realize that I was just a pawn in his game of complacency. Was I too naïve to notice? What woman would not appreciate hearing that she was *naturally beautiful*? That she did not need to wear make-up? What a nice compliment, right?

"Wrong," my aunt said. "It was part of his plan to get no one else to look at you."

She had a point and his plan had worked. Never before in my entire life had I dressed so casually.

That afternoon, we continued our aimless search for sea glass on a beach where there wasn't any. He always walked way ahead of me or way behind me, but never with me. As we walked in silence, I wondered why each and every rock on the beach was shaped the same, flat and oval. I had no explanation as to why, but I ascertained it had something to do with the same reason we found very little sea glass on the Rhode Island beaches. Perhaps it was just indicative of harsh waves on a rocky shore.

There was little glass, few shells, yet a plentiful amount of gorgeous oval shaped stones. As we continued our walk, something caught my eye. I picked it up. It was white and oval shaped just like every other stone on the beach, but it was much thinner and did not seem to be made of rock.

I squinted at it, then looked at it from different angles. I held it in my hand trying hard to figure out what it was. I handed it to him and he could not tell what it was either. I turned it over and over in my hand caressing its iridescent mother of pearl qualities.

Suddenly I knew. Though it no longer resembled it, it was not stone, but a shell. Lengthened and now only a few centimeters wide, it had been beaten down. What was once a beautiful shell somehow became pummeled into the exact shape of the millions of stones strewn across the shoreline. Was it the destiny of anything that neared this water; to be shaped and molded into an oval form?

That night I had a dream. I was in Bridgeport on my favorite glass collecting beach. In the dream, I was collecting sea glass with the actor Ryan

Gosling. He smiled at me as he helped me put the tempered glass into my bright yellow bucket. We walked down the beach together, my hand in his. The dream was so vivid that even the sensation of walking through sand, the labored drawl, so slow and deliberate felt real. *Finally,* my boyfriend had been replaced with a more handsome and successful man, *in my dreams at least.* I tried to forget about the whole thing, and instead tried resuscitate our lifeless relationship.

Less than a month later, he almost killed me in a violent rage. We were staying overnight at a hotel when he lost his mind and entrapped me in our room. From behind, he picked me up and effortlessly threw me across the floor. With at least a hundred pounds on my demure frame, he held me down on the bed with ease. Cuffing my wrists in his hands, he repeatedly screamed into my face for me to shut up.

Terrified, I screamed at the top of my lungs. Angered by my lack of compliance, he threatened me, "If you don't shut the fuck up, I'm going to head butt you in the face and break your fuckin' teeth."

This only made me scream louder.

"No! I like my teeth!" I cried.

"Shut the fuck up!" he yelled.

But even when I did, when I did *shut the fuck up,* he continued to berate me by screaming into my face to *shut the fuck up.* Still pinning me down, I writhed underneath him and struggled to free my hands, but he was just too strong.

Then my heart nearly burst out of my chest when he put a pillow over my face. I could not breath. My pulse raced in unison with my thoughts. Moments ago I had pleaded with God, with the angels, and whomever else who could hear my prayers to send someone to save me, to send someone to get me out of there, but no one had arrived. Now he pressed a pillow firmly against my nose and mouth. With every passing second I thought about the daughter of our dry cleaner, who was murdered by her boyfriend when he was away on a vacation.

The story itself was a horrific, how he discarded her body was atrocious. Unlike myself, I do not think she even made it into her twenties. Here I was in a hotel room with a pillow cutting off my air supply and all I could think about was her. I had always assumed what happened to her was one of those things that only happens to *other people*... something that would never happen to me. It just did not seem possible or probable. Maybe it was just youthful ignorance, that feeling of immortality that eventually corrects itself with age and experience; as it undoubtedly corrected itself that night.

Those few seconds that passed felt more like minutes. With the pillow still over my mouth, I felt like Andromeda, chained to a rock in the middle of the ocean as the sea monster closed in on her. Everything stopped in that moment; would she be saved or would she be destroyed? Now, all I could think of was the phone call my parents would be getting the next morning that their daughter was found dead in the a hotel room somewhere in the middle of upstate New York.

Suddenly he pulled the pillow off of my face. We stared at each other in shock. I do not think either one of us could believe what he had done.

"Do you know what you just did?" I demanded.

He began to get angry at me again, so I calmly tried to talk him down, "How would your family feel. What would your mother think if she knew about what you just did to me?"

The guilt trip seemed to work. Though he still simmered, I was brazen. I was angry too! I continued with the bit about his family until I convinced him to free my arms.

"Okay," he obliged. "I will let go of you if you promise not to go anywhere."

I smiled reassuringly and nodded in agreement. As soon as he let go of me, I jumped off the bed, dashed for the door, and yanked it open. So close behind me, with one seamless gesture he slammed it shut. Seething, he started to scream again and pushed me onto the ground. Like a prisoner, I leaned my head longingly against the only escape route, a solid metal door, as he held it shut.

There was no end to his rage. *When would he stop?* I wondered. Here I was in a beautiful gown, jewelery, and make-up. He wore a gorgeous tuxedo and looked amazing.

How and why would someone transform what could have been a beautiful night into a nightmare? Weak both emotionally and physically, I just wanted to curl up into a ball. I thought of Sandy, my stuffed animal from my childhood. I wanted to lay down and cuddle with her and sleep for a long long time. I no longer had the energy to fight, in fact I never had. He continued to shout. I sunk farther and farther into the floor as he towered over me.

Then someone unexpectedly knocked on the door. I looked at him surprised.

"You better open it," I said slyly as they knocked again.

"What if it's the cops? If you don't open it you might get in even more trouble."

He slowly backed away from the door and allowed me enough space to stand up from the ground. I smoothed my dress as I rose. He composed himself and I turned the door handle.

The door opened and I recognized the face of the front desk manager. He looked embarrassed to have witnessed this disgrace.

"Please let me out!" I begged and squeezed through the slightly jarred doorway.

The people across the hall stood outside of their room and flagged me into it. They must have heard the whole thing. I knew for sure they had witnessed part of what happened earlier that night. They too were at the wedding and were related to his friends. His friends would never know the truth, and if they did, they would not believe it. A few even saw what happened in the hallway, before we entered the room; when he first threatened to hurt me.

"I'm going to headbutt you in the fuckin' face," he screamed, pushing his face so close into mine that every time he spoke his spit entered my mouth.

"What?" I responded confused by this sudden threat of violence. As I backed away from him, he continued to walk forward to fill the gap between us.

"Give me the fuckin' key!" he demanded.

I furiously dug through my large purse. I looked for it, but at the same time, tried to keep an eye on him afraid he might follow through with his threat and head butt me in the face.

Earlier in the night, I tried to get away. When we reached our floor, I jumped back into the elevator and tried to escape, but he followed closely behind me. I was terrified at the prospects of being alone with him in that small confined space had its door trapped us inside.

Now I was about to enter the hotel room with him, but only because I wanted to make sure he did not destroy my belongings.

"You're so fuckin' stupid that you can't even find the Goddamn room key," he roared.

Eventually I found the key and nervously looked behind me as I opened the door. Like fog rolling slowly above the ocean's surface, I could feel the anger rising off of him. In silence, I walked into the room and sat at a desk chair far away from where he stood. I tried to keep my distance, but he snuck up on me and threw the desk chair across the room with me in it. The chair and I flew across the quarters, and then he picked me up, like a rag doll, and threw me onto the bed. Then he did the unspeakable, he put a pillow over my face. I could not breath; things began to close in around me.

I will never forget how often he said that I was heartless. I suppose I was cold at times, but I did try to love him. With his unpredictable personality and rage issues, he was a difficult person to like let alone love.

After I escaped the room and hid in the other room, with the door cracked, I watched from across the hall. The woman in the room next to ours came out. He still stood in front of our hotel room with some sort of dumbfounded expression. Dressed in a housecoat with a head full of curlers she scolded him loudly for waking her up. As she shook her finger at him and crossed her arms, I thought to myself that perhaps she was my angel, *the one who posed the noise complaint.*

He apologized profusely to her and acted like the most perfect of gentlemen. Kindly, he offered to cover the cost of her room even though he was barely able to pay for ours. *What an asshole,* I thought.

I admit that I did not leave even after he tried to kill me, but I did leave eventually. One of the last times we spoke, he looked despondent as he sat on his bedroom floor and he leaned up against his nightstand. Being the glutton for punishment I could not help but ask,

"Have you already replaced me?"

"I could never replace you," he answered.

What he said echoed in my ears. It was not what he said but the way he said it as if just the thought of someone else measuring up to me *pained* him. He always treated me like I was nothing, yet I knew he thought I was beautiful and kind, he told me often, and sometimes he also told me that he was a monster.

"If you love me so much then why did you do this?"

"*Me?* You've caused every fight we've ever had!"

"Are you kidding? You can't blame me for *your* actions. Your actions were your choice-- no one made you do anything."

This angered him.

Every time he flew into a rage, he blamed me for being the catalyst. He could make anything my fault. I never took the blame and was perceptive enough to know that he was responsible for his own actions. Every time he yelled and swore in my face, I said very little back.

"How can you blame *me* for the way *you're* acting?" I had ask, "Don't you think I want to scream and swear at you right now? But I'm not."

Again, he would blame me and cite that I was the only person in his entire life that made him this angry. He would say that he could not control himself and that when this happened, it was like another person took over, that this loss of control was unpredictable. Now, I saw through his bullshit.

One minute, I was crouched down on the dirty floor of a hotel room fearing for my life and not more than a few seconds later, he was playing nice guy again and kissing the old woman in the next room's ass. He knew *exactly* what he was doing. This was the most evil and manipulative person I had ever met and finally I realized that I was just a pawn, part of some elaborate fabrication constructed in his mind.

In the past, he cried to me several times as he tried to make sense of his actions. *Why did he treat the person he loved so much so badly?* That is what he would wonder.

In retrospect, he might have thought I was beautiful and kind, but he certainly did not love me. I was just a trophy to him, something he prized so highly that he did not ever want anyone to see it.

So confused by it all, I thought he meant it, that he loved me. I did not know I was being abused, though it was clear that *I was being abused.* Hearing loss, backing me into a wall screaming, pushing me. It all led up to the night that he almost killed me. Somehow I did not see it coming; it was the facade. He had me and everyone else fooled. He was so kind to my family and to strangers. Every one of his friend's moms loved him, as he always offered to help in the kitchen. He was Mr. Nice Guy, Mr. All American blond-haired blue-eyed fraud.

In the world, it seems there are some lucky ones who find their soul mate in the first person they date. I know a few of those people. They are happy, yet cannot quench a part of life that they will never obtain. Their homes, car payments, and children keep them bound to mostly suburban areas. They yearn to travel to far-off places, to experience the freedom they once or never had, to be a free spirit and explore who they were --- or who they might be minus their worldly attachments, their children, spouse, and home.

The majority of them will wonder, but never know. While the free spirits, those who have loved and lost and have secured almost no attachment, view them with a sense of disdain. *Why would anyone want those kind of lives,* they wonder, disgusted mainly by the conformity of it all, especially the minivans and prefabricated neighborhoods. Until one day, on their unsuspecting path, they meet and fall in love with someone who takes their heart and smashes it again and again until it splinters into millions of pieces, pulverizing it.

It is on that day that the free spirit learns something new: they begin to understand why people want to get married because they too now yearn collectively for one thing; the day someone walks into their lives, promises never to leave, and actually means it.

The night was clear and full of stars. Outside I leaned against my porch, hidden away from the world, where no one could find me.

"I want to come see you," I whispered into my cell phone.

"I don't think that's a good idea," he replied.

"Why? I *need* to see you."

"I just can't."

"Why not?"

"I just can't. I can't bare to see you drive away again."

"Then don't look."

"I have to."

"No. You don't *have to* do anything. You don't have to watch."

"Yes I do."

"No you don't."

"Yes I do."

"Why?"

"It's like with the sea glass; when I didn't want to go with you because it hurt my neck too much to look for it. I would go with you anyways, just so you could collect glass and in the end, when we got there I always ended up looking for the glass anyways, *even though I originally said I wouldn't.* And it always ended up hurting my neck."

The next morning, I had a dream I was on Daytona Beach. The sand was much more yellow, a more warmly lit hue than I remembered, more reminiscent of the very last photograph I took on Misquamicut Beach in Rhode Island. Standing next to me was a childhood friend who I had not spoken to in years. I was telling her about how in Florida you could see wild dolphins in the water and then, as soon as I had spoken those words, very close to the shoreline, a lone dolphin appeared.

"Look! A dolphin," I said and pointed excitedly.

III

Venus

Hunting he loved, but love he laugh'd to scorn-

At first, I counted the days that we did not speak. After day seven, I began to lose track. My thoughts began to revolve around an empty factory building near his house, a large industrial giant, that stretched on for at least a quarter mile.

On my way to his place, the building often captured my imagination as I drove by. The city itself, Waterbury, Connecticut, was like the empty factory buildings that encompassed its landscape, longstanding abandoned remnants of the industrial era.

As a child, I felt a sense of dread every time we drove by one of these many long forgotten manufacturing hubs; not because they were empty, but because they were once full. I know why they call a shell a shell. Once it was a living breathing animal, a mollusk with a protective exoskeleton, but then the life inside of it died; that's when it became a shell.

We took our last trip to Rhode Island a few weeks before we broke up. That afternoon, we ended up on Misquamicut Beach. It was a beautiful day that anyone would appreciate, anyone but him, of course. He was reluctant to be there; I had to beg him to take me. We walked through the sand and as always, he walked a few steps ahead of me or behind me but never with me. Intermittently blowing through my hair, the wind was the only element that animated the scenery on this blustery spring day as we traversed the shore in silence. That day, the sense of disconnect and empty nostalgia could only be reproduced had the event been filmed by an old 8mm camera and silently played across a dark living room wall.

It was already chilly and soon the sun would start to slink slowly in the sky. I regretted not bringing my sweat shirt, though not enough to complain about it for fear he might get angry and demand we go back to the car, thus forfeiting my opportunity to walk the beach and look for glass.

In the distance we spotted a group of people crowding around something and posing in front of it to take pictures. From afar, neither of us could tell what it was. I feared the worst. A beached mammal perhaps? But why would anyone take pictures of themselves with a suffering or possibly dead animal? The idea alone was morbid. As we got closer a large pile of sticks came into focus.

From far away, the mound of sticks appeared to be massive. *That's weird.* Who would take the time out of their busy day to neatly pile together a mountain of sticks on the middle of a beach? We discussed the thought and proceeded forward. Neither of us could figure out what mystery awaited us until we stood in front of it. We were stunned by our discovery.

It was not a pile of sticks but roots, roots of entire tree that shot out in every direction like the spray of a whale. We stood in awe of it. What was once a large uprooted tree had been transformed into a huge piece of driftwood. A silent beauty resonated from its muted gray tones as it sat unmoving against the quiet surf that perpetually rolled in one wave at a time.

He wanted me to take a picture of him with it. He walked over and climbed onto its trunk standing tall and proud to pose for the shot. Something in this action appalled me; the human disruption of a peaceful castaway of unknown origin. It was as if he had spit on sacred ground. He was not supposed to be there standing upon this tree to pose for a snapshot. Reluctantly, I took the picture as the surf continued to roll onto the shore, the sea foam bubbled like champagne as it receded back into the water.

Even after we moved on and continued to comb the beach for sea glass, I kept wondering where the tree had come from. That year, violent storms ripped

through the seasons, tornados and hurricanes destroyed both land and shore

without discrimination. Could it have traveled north from the Carolinas where

hurricanes slammed into the beaches earlier that year?

My mind tried to make sense of its arrival and created logical scenarios to

explain it, but I conceded. It would be a subject bundled together with all the other

things in life that could not be compartmentalized or known.

I thought about its colors, the trunk was stark white in some places. How

long had it been laying in the sun, hollow and lifeless? How could something so

dead be so beautiful?

As we walked on, something purple glimmered in the sand and caught

my eye. I snatched it. At first I thought it was a piece of sea glass. Its color

gradient differed from the lilac sea glass I had seen before; glass that was usually

one solid color. This piece was deep purple on one end and faded gradually from

dark purple to lilac to opaque white. This was not a piece of glass, it was amethyst,

a piece of *sea amethyst,* tempered and smoothed into the shape of a perfect tear

drop.

Though it was not yet summer, that was one of our last visits to the beach.

After we broke up, I feared that it would be a beachless summer for me, not

because he had a beach house and we were no longer on speaking terms, but

because I had no one to go to the beach with. I feared that my summer would be

spent watching the season fade away, leaves turning from green to shades of

amber, from the window of my inland residence.

What he did to me left me feeling lethargic and void, like the woman in

Gauguin's painting *Loss of Virginity.*

There was nothing beautiful about that painting. To me, it seemed that it truly was a loss in the sense that something had been taken. *Stolen.* The subject of the painting is a woman who lies supine flimsily grasping a wilting violet. Her facial expression indicates mourning. This is how he left me feeling.

At that moment, I promised myself I would never let a man make me a means to an end again. The thought of him alone disgusted me. How had I ended up with someone who disgusted me? How had I let him touch me? How had I let him inside? Like a shipwrecked sailor, lost at sea for years, I was unsure which navigational folly brought me so far from my intended destination.

My childhood had been one of sadness. My life at school was not much better. For a large part of it, I was bullied: some sort of social outcast. Until high school when I met *him.* I remember the first time our eyes met. Electricity shot from my head to the rest of my body. He smiled and said "Hi."

Nervously I smiled back holding fast to his glance until he passed by. *I was thrilled.*

I knew dating him was a bad idea. That he was a bad boy, but I was no stranger to danger. I was starved for it, for love. My life up to that point had been reckless, full of partying and drugs, but love was something that had always alluded me. I was damaged. I had been raped and never spoke of it. My mind was in a constant state of stress and confusion. My home life was turbulent. The relationship with him, though abusive, was my release. When I was with him, I felt like I never had before: I fell whole.

It started off good, *well sort of.* He lied to me to trick me into sleeping with him. I found out about it from his buddy many months later that he had planned to just sleep with me and then leave me, but for some reason, he stayed. *Maybe he did love me.*

During the first summer we were together, he would pick me up from work at a local cafe where I waitressed. We would drive off to the beach as the sun set late in the evening sky. On the beach, he laid a blanket down, and kissed me. It was where our relationship began; where he first told me he loved me. Easily, he coerced me to take off my jeans.

Sometimes we would stay at the beach until sunrise, but only when we were fighting; only if he had broken up with me. I would refuse to get into the car, then sit on the rocky ledge and cry. Tears streamed down my face and into the sea.

He was not very apologetic. Usually, he would break up with me, then he would ask me back out.

At the beach, he would tell me that he was sorry and that he did not really mean it, that he really did not want to break up with me just to get me in the car. And as soon as the passenger door closed and locked, he would break up with me again. From the car window, I would watch the gulls fly into the air then float slowly back down to the Earth like angels as orange rays shot through the sky announcing the morning.

In the beginning, I tried hard to avoid going out with him. After the first time we hung out, I ignored him, but no matter how much I ignored him, I could not forget him. His broad muscular chest, his smiling Irish eyes, though they were brown like mine, they were extremely sexy. It was as if my heart had made its choice before I was ever presented with one.

Up until that point, with all the the torment and teasing I had been through, even rape, no one had ever defended me. I sought safety and security and thought I finally found this kind of protection in his masculinity, but he was only a man on the surface. Regardless of the truth, I fell as hard as Venus did for Adonis when Cupid's arrow accidentally pierced her heart.

When we were not fighting everything about him was amazing and romantic. And without prompting, he always sent me roses. He was passionate and the only person who ever sent chills through my body when we kissed, "Did you feel that?" he would ask.

It was not just me. He felt it too.

At first, Venus tried to stop herself from loving Adonis, but she could not resist him; the gash from Cupid's arrow was too deep a wound and her love for him reflected this. Perhaps Venus had tried to avoid the love affair because she too sensed it would end in tragedy.

I was at the nail salon waiting for my acrylics to dry when my cell phone rang. It was him and in his voice I sensed urgency.

"We need to talk, *like right now*," he said.

"Talk about what?" Instantly, I knew, "You cheated on me didn't you?"

He did not answer me and told me to come to his house. I quickly paid the nail technician and ran out the door to my car where I wailed like a pathetic baby until wailing eventually graduated to hyperventilation. My nail polish got smudged and scratched as I fumbled with my car keys. I finally turned the ignition

and shifted. Wiping tears away as I drove, I sped to his house. I knew that once I

got there that everything would be ruined, including my nails.

He sometimes disappeared for a day or three. This often happened during

the time between breaking up and getting back together. This last time we broke

up, things were different. He would disappear for a whole weekend. Frustrated

after not hearing from him for three days, like Venus seeking out Adonis as he

hunted deep in the woods, I went to his favorite bar hoping to run into him. I

walked in, his back was turned to me, but his black leather jacket was

unmistakable. There he was. I tapped him on his shoulder while glaring at his best

friend's skanky bleached-blond girlfriend seated on the barstool beside him.

Once Venus found Adonis in the woods, she warned him to stay away

from the dangerous animals, like lions and bears: the ones that could overtake him,

and encouraged him to hunt the smaller ones instead, like hares and foxes. She

loved him and did not want to see him get hurt, or worse, "Be brave towards the

timid; courage against the courageous is not safe. Beware how you expose

yourself to danger, and put my happiness to risk. Attack not the beasts that Nature

has armed with weapons."

During the time we were together, I had plenty of reason to suspect that

he cheated on me, but I did not want to believe it. I often came across scraps of

paper with phone numbers scribbled across them. When we went out to dinner, he

accepted waitresses' phone numbers while I was in the bathroom. It disgusted me

that the waitresses were rude enough to flirt with him right in front of me as we ate.

Another time I found a pink sock in his laundry. I was sure I had caught him that time, that was until his mother claimed that the tiny sock was hers. He was brazen in his disrespect of me, often standing me up and never coming home when he said he would only to come back with the complexion of a ghost and the inability to articulate words.

After warning Adonis, Venus took her swan-drawn chariot and flew away. Adonis, too arrogant to take Venus' words into consideration, plodded onwards for the kill. Unknowingly, his dogs had awoken a wild bore who tore through the forest. When it made itself known, Adonis threw a spear at the animal, but failed to fatally wound it. The beast, now angry, tackled Adonis, pinned him to the ground, and impaled him with his tusks.

That night at the bar, we left as a couple. It was raining and before driving off, we stalled in the car and kissed passionately as Whitney Houston's "I Have Nothing" played on the radio. I will never forget that moment. Every time we were away from each other, regardless of circumstance, when we met up again, when we kissed, it was just as intense as the first time we were together. I understood, in a way, how women could stay with men who cheated, even if they were married to them. It is hard to leave the person you love no matter what they do, until the day the pain starts to outweigh the love.

When we got home, he took me into his arms and into his bedroom, but something felt different. His passion, our connection, was lost. It completely disappeared and was replaced with an emotionless insensitivity that was not him. I pushed him off of me and began to sob uncontrollably. Typically he would have been pissed that I refused sex, let alone pushed him off of me in the middle of it, but this time he cowered over me concerned for my well-being. I ignored him and cried into his pillow.

He watched me sob in disbelief, "Why are you crying? What's wrong?" he asked me in a gentle voice, kind of like how game fisherman only present their best bait in the tightest sporting conditions.

"Please tell me what's wrong," he said brushing strands of my tear soaked hair off of my face.

Venus, still on her way to Cyprus, instantly knew when Adonis had fallen. *She felt it.* Immediately, she turned her chariot around and descended back into the forest, but his soul was already gone. Just his body lay waiting for her; *a shell.*

"I don't know what's wrong. Something felt different."

He looked at me wide-eyed as he petted my hair. He was terrified. Terrified I would find out whatever secret he had been trying to keep, though somehow my body already knew.

That afternoon, by the time I had arrived at his house, everything I thought I had was gone. He had already spoken to the girl and they corroborated on a story to tell me. I knew her. She was one of my friends. He handed me the phone, "It was a special kiss, Hayley" she said.

Venus came upon him and held his lifeless body in a close embrace. Avenging the Gods of his death, she sprinkled nectar over his blood. Raindrops began to fall and bubble. Beneath the blood he shed, a purple flower sprouted from the ground. The swan-drawn chariot carried Venus away back into the sky. The flower, an anemone, was frail and required a zephyr to blow its blossom open, yet so delicate that after it bloomed the slightest gust of wind could just as easily blow all its petals away.

"You're full of shit!" I screamed into the phone and threw it at him.

He tried to stop me as I ran toward the door.

"Don't touch me! Let go of me!" I shouted and sobbed in unison. "How could you do this to me? I loved you!"

There was no *special kiss*. It was a lie. The only reason he told me about her was because she started to show up at his house uninvited and leave letters in his mailbox. Though she had her own boyfriend, she wanted mine and had been following him everywhere, even showing up unexpectedly at his gym.

Then I got the details about what really happened. One night, my boyfriend and a buddy met up with her and one of her girlfriends. The four of them shared a cheap motel room in town. He hooked up with her while his friend hooked up with the other girl. *Classy.*

I never told anyone that we were secretly engaged. He had asked me to marry him that Valentine's Day, got down on one knee and everything. Somewhere in my soul I knew it would never happen and that it was best that we did not make it down the aisle or more likely to City Hall. No one knew about it, even though I wore a diamond ring. I did not ever tell my parents; they hated him.

Sometimes at picnics relatives would ask about the ring, "Is that an engagement ring?"

"No," I would lie.

Yes, I wanted to scream. *Yes* it was, and *yes* he loved me!

The big problem I was having now was that cheap motel, *the motor inn.* I had to drive by it every time I left my house because I lived down the street from it. It was not just a motel; it was the crime scene where my heart was brutalized by my callous cheating fiancée. In one violent motion, it was ripped from my chest leaving some huge gaping hole that could never be filled.

Sometimes just driving by it made me cry. As I passed, I would turn my head and stare at it the way they warn you not to stare when you pass car wrecks or other tragedies. In my mind, the Wolcott Motor Inn was still surrounded with caution tape. Beyond the tape there were no outlines of bodies; just one chalk outline of a lonely broken heart.

Regardless of what had happened between us, it was difficult to get past this love and even harder to find anything like it ever again, *not that I was looking.* Perhaps love was just an illusion; something that some couples sustained better than others. My heart's chalk outline in the parking lot, once bright white, was now faded, washed away by the rain. The pain of missing him and having to drive by the motel daily stretched on for months until one day he unexpectedly showed up at my front door.

Venus's relationship with Adonis ended in death, as does any romance. A relationship in demise is a death sentence of the heart. Even if paroled, the love from the beginning of the pairing can never be regained, obtained, or even imitated.

For the next two weeks, he took me everywhere. We both seemed happy to be together again; he showered me with attention and gifts. Perhaps he was making up for what had never been between us. He took me to Salem, Massachusetts because the history of the Salem Witch Trials interested me, and more so because I liked looking at all different herbs, stones and potions in the modern day witch's apothecary shops. We spent the afternoon in downtown Salem, walking around, visiting all of my favorite stores, and dined at a local seafood restaurant. As the evening began to escape us, we debated whether or not we should go back to Connecticut.

That night, we stayed overnight in an ancient castle by the sea or *at least a hotel that looked like one.* I could not wait until we were alone. I felt electricity every time we kissed; every time he touched me. Just being with him felt more right than anytime I was alone, especially when I was sleeping. Without him, I could not sleep and during the months he was gone, I slept encased in pillows to give myself some false sense or feeling that he was still there.

The next morning, we went to the wharf of the fishing village of Gloucester where ancient fishing nets and buoys decorated the businesses and boat houses alike. We walked to the dock. From a distance, the smaller boats bobbed and swayed in the water like toy boats floating in a bathtub. We walked down the gangway and onto a large boat. In the two years we were together he constantly refused, but for some reason on this day he had finally agreed to take me on a whale watch.

He had never been whale-watching before. That morning in anticipation, I threw on a sweatshirt and visor and purchased a disposable camera for the outing. Though I was enjoying all the time we were spending together, I could not ignore the feeling our time together gave me. It was like any day at the beach as a child. It was well past mid-afternoon and although you were still wading in the ocean, you had a sense that any moment your mother would be yelling at you to get out of the water; it was time to go home and there was nothing you could do about it.

I snapped pictures of him as the boat began its journey out to sea. He smiled and took the camera out of my hand. I posed playfully with a huge grin on my face, then pulled him close to me and turned the camera on both of us. I had to conserve *some* film for the whales, though it was a boring hour and a half before we saw any wildlife. Soon we saw lots. We saw fins and tails, as the whales surfaced. He was impressed; I was disappointed. The last time I had been whale watching the whales were breaching. This time we saw maybe one breach.

I took several more pictures. After the trip, now late in the afternoon, we decided to drive back to Connecticut. On the way home, his phone rang. It was his best friend's girlfriend, that skanky blond, again. After saying "Hello," he quickly blurted out the following:

"I can't talk right now, Hayley's with me."

I will never forget those words because they were not just words but the verbal equivalent of shattering my truck's windows or cutting off my air supply. It was over. It was time to cremate the relationship and scatter its ashes back into the sea from which it was born.

For weeks, the disposable camera sat on my desk. I contemplated its fate. The thought of developing and viewing the pictures of us together that last time was excruciatingly painful. One afternoon in a fit of rage, I took the camera out to the garage. I sobbed as I smashed it to pieces with my grandfather's hammer and threw its lifeless body, pieces of plastic twisted in film, into the trash can. Like the photographs that preserved the memories of that day, he was gone forever and with him he took my heart.

It was no secret how I ended up alone on this deserted island. I had chartered the destination to go off course long ago: right after *he* walked out of my life or I out of his. Carelessly, I surrendered the control of the hull to the wiles of the sea to do with it as they saw fit. I dated people I was only half interested in and altogether avoided the ones that sent crazy vibrations up my spine. After all these failed relationships, I still wondered how I had inevitably arrived on the shores of

Rhode Island with *him,* a man who repulsed me. Soon the answer became clear. I had experienced love, that's how, and after the love was gone, I promised myself I would never let something that painful happen to me. *Never again.*

Like Scarlett O'Hara, Vivien Leigh's character from *Gone With the Wind,* I stopped feeling; it was the perfect defense mechanism to keep myself from getting hurt. I began to understand her character's emotional vacancy. It worked well for keeping people out, but usually what attracts a person to someone is the very thing that one day becomes its downfall.

It was more than that. I did not want anything serious. I was afraid of being domesticated. I knew what happened when wild animals were tamed; they called it *breaking* for a reason. I could stay in those relationships, but not forever. They were safe like the artificial environment of a dolphin in captivity; their tanks lacked natural predators and had more than enough nourishment to sustain them; all at the cost of freedom.

For the most part, I expected to swim in and out of these relationships unscathed. I did not realize how soon they could escalate and become violent. I almost died. Even before he almost took my life, I understood why we did not mesh: I had not loved him. It was not until we broke up that I realized that despite his claims, he had not loved me either. Back then, I still felt safer in a dead end romance than letting my heart roam free in the wild. There were few predators in my carefully-controlled environment, *or at least that's what I thought.*

I never felt anything for him that was not forced. Brainwashed and thinking he was desperately in love with me, I did not protest when he called me names like "cold-hearted" and "heartless" because I felt that I deserved them. He made it seem like his love was so real while mine was not good enough.

Those names, *heartless* and *cold-hearted*, felt more like titles, birthrights, that I did not have the right of disputing. They stuck in my head long after we broke up and I believed them. His words broke my confidence. Would I never truly be able to love or feel love again? Was I broken? I feared that somehow I was reduced to a Scarlett O'Hara, *an indisputable ice queen.* I no longer worried about being cold-hearted, I *feared* it. Maybe he was right. If *he* could not love me, then who would? From what he said, I was so frigid that no man would ever want anything to do with me again.

With him gone, I began to realize that there were a lot of things I feared. When we were together, I received an abnormal result on my gynecological exam. I had never had anything like that happen before. Immediately, I glared at him wondering if he had been cheating. The nurse told me it was not a big deal and that I needed to retest in six months. Now, it was almost six months later and the test date was coming up. I would have to walk into the doctor's office by myself and find out my test results alone, too.

A few weeks after our break-up, I ended up back on the ocean. For days prior, I wondered if I would ever see it again. Would I be doomed to spend my oceanless summer solitarily because I had nobody to go with? One thing was for certain: I would never be able to go to my favorite sea glass collecting destination by myself. I was terrified to walk the beach alone; even during the day in a city with as high of a murder rate as Bridgeport's.

A few weeks passed and I slowly began to heal. I went back out into the world with more confidence than I ever had before. I did not need a relationship and could for once rely on myself. I planned to finish my novella and if that did not work out, get a nine to five job until I figured out what to do next.

A friend even suggested I take a year or two off from dating. Two years of no cuddling, no kissing, and no sex? Well, I guess I could manage. With this last boyfriend, I did not want to do any of those things and I still was not feeling like myself, so what did it matter? But soon my plans began to crumble just as thin ice first cracks ominously before breaking. On my first night back to the ocean, I met a man.

That night had been peculiar. My cousin and I went to a bar in Niantic and sat at a table next to two overweight middle-aged women. One of the women was pleasant to talk to while the other was a belligerent drunk who continuously tripped over her slurs.

A few guys walked onto the patio where we sat. It was a sunny day. We looked them over from afar, one was fair and blond, the other was very dark. Soon the nicer of the two drunk ladies started talking to us and bummed a cigarette off my cousin. She pointed to the two guys while she smoked,"My, my they are cute!"

She winked at me then flagged them over. *Oh geez.* They reluctantly sauntered on by.

"Kiss my, hand, " she demanded, shoving it into the fairer one's face. He politely obliged.

"Kiss it again" she demanded.

What a bitch! My cousin and I could not stop giggling. The group of us chatted as he lit up a smoke. The woman, still unable to keep her hands off of him pulled the cigarette out of his mouth, took a long drag off of it and put it back between his lips.

"You two just practically made out," I laughed.

He shot me a dirty look.

"We have to get going," the woman said, "Hopefully we'll run into you later." She winked at him then named a few of the bars she might be at before exiting.

We introduced ourselves to the guys. The blond had the same name as my first ex boyfriend, the one who had really broken my heart.

"Oh great," I whispered to my cousin.

My cousin was a few years younger than me, but sometimes made a lot of sense.

"It really doesn't matter that they have the same name," she replied.

True. I thought. They sat down at the table with us. The blond said he raced bikes in Daytona.

"Professionally?" I asked.

"*With* professionals," he replied.

He sat next to me and told me a little about his life. He was a fireman. His sister owned a sweet shop, and the more beer he drank, the more he insisted on bringing us there to see it.

I did not instantly fall for him, but as the night went on, I started to. Between him and my cousin, I could not stop laughing and had not laughed that much in over a year. What just days ago I considered a badly wounded heart began to heal. My heart was not cold, *only when I was with my previous boyfriend.* Sitting next to this stranger, I felt something that I had not felt in a long time.

What my ex said still bothered and worried me. Part of the reason I did not want to date anyone new was because I feared that he was right: that I was not only coldhearted, but heartless. I had believed everything he said and that somehow, over the years I had conditioned myself to be that way.

That night, my heart began to feel warm again. The entire night, I could not stop smiling. How could my ex call me heartless? Every time he said it, I felt like he had stabbed me right in the chest. But now I could feel and it did not take much for my heart to start working again. Suddenly I realized that he was wrong-that those names were all just part of the abuse. I was not heartless. I had never been. He was heartless and for too long, I had let him define me.

Earlier in the night, I had experienced such intense *deja vu* that it almost drove me to calling my ex. As I was getting weak and ready to pick up my phone, the very idea of calling him was intervened by me meeting this new guy. It was as if he was an angel that swooped down just in time to save me. Though another relationship was the farthest thing from my mind, *they* do say that when you are not looking for a relationship is when love decides to show up.

The sun went down as the band wrapped up. We decided it was time to meet with our older lady friends. He, however, continued to insist we go to the sweet shop and then maybe to his beach house.

My cousin, now drunk, had no interest in going to a candy store, "Do they have beer there?" she whined.

The entire way there, she announced over and over again that she "wanted a sucker."

We walked into the brightly lit store.

"Take whatever you want," he said and went into the back room.

The candy store looked like a *candy store*. It was filled with every type of sweet you could imagine. Little cubbies covered the wall, filled with salt water taffy of every flavor. And there were big jars filled with suckers of all kinds. We stood around the candy shop waiting for him to come back into the room.

"Here," I said, and handed her a lollipop.

"I don't want it," she said as she took it out of my hand and threw it back into the bucket.

"You said you wanted a sucker!"

"*I was joking.*"

"Well I don't want anything either," I said, feeling a little awkward standing in the middle of the candy store at eleven o'clock on a Saturday night.

"Let's just take a one each and that's it. *I don't want him to feel bad.*"

"Yeah, whatever. Where the hell is he? I want to go back to the bar."

He came out from the back room.

"That's all you took?" he said, as we walked out of the store. I shook my head yes.

"No!" my cousin interjected, "When you weren't looking I stuffed fistfuls of Jolly Ranchers and gumdrops into my pockets!"

We crossed the street and walked towards one of the bars where the women told us to meet them. We went inside, but they were not there. We walked a couple blocks to the next bar to look for the women. This next bar was a real dive. We walked in and looked all around.

"They're not here," said my cousin.

"Hold on," I said and walked to the back room. They were not there. I found it odd that after they hooked me up with this guy, they disappeared into thin air. As days went by, I began to realize that our meeting may have been a miraculous one. I may not have spoken to him at such lengths had the women not shoved him in my direction. On top of that, the fact that I met him on the only night that I was planning on being down by the shore was peculiar. Even more interestingly was the fact that he only stayed at his beach house a few weeks out of the year and that night just happened to fall into this time frame.

Based on the most standard clichéd principles, it seemed that our meeting was meant to be. I started to think that my sad ending with the monster was not such a sad ending after all. Maybe I would have someone to go to the beach with this summer, someone who would look for sea glass with me, and someone who might hold my hand when I got my test result back. Maybe we had broken up for a reason; maybe so I could live happily ever after with someone else. Maybe him? I did not want any more or any less than anyone else wanted. I just wanted someone to love, someone who would love me back.

We gave up looking for the women and went back to the original bar just as another band was setting up. It was getting late, but we were still having a lot of fun. He insisted on bringing us to his beach house.

"I'll make you guys something to eat and then show you the ocean."

My cousin rolled her eyes,"We've already seen it --- plenty of times, thank-you anyways."

"Well Hayley said she was writing a book about it," what he said was true.

"You're just tryin' to get some!" My cousin countered...

He ignored her and played with his phone, he was in the middle of writing a text.

"He's not going to get any," I said to my cousin. " Not from *me,* at least."

He quickly looked up from what he was doing.

"Not gonna get any *from you?* What is that suppose to mean?"

"Well, I cannot say definitively that you aren't going to ge*t any* at all, tonight. I mean, I do not know who you're texting or if you're gonna get any from *them,*" I laughed.

He tried to act insulted, but even he could not stop laughing, none of us could.

Back at his monstrous three-story beach house, he threw some beers and a bottle of $50 sake in a cooler, then carried it over to his neighbor's. We ended up at the backyard bonfire where we joined ten or more college-aged kids who lounged around the fire in lawn chairs. I felt old and wondered if they were even legal.

"Do you mind if I take her to the beach for a few minutes?" he said to my cousin, who was fairly inebriated at this point.

"I don't care what you do, as long as you leave that cooler with me."

We walked over to the water. The cool sand slid through my sandals and past the soles of my feet. Not another person was on the beach at that hour. The hollowness of the empty shore was amplified by the monotonous sound of waves as they gently swished in and out of the sea. The light from the far off breakwater flashed as we walked silently down the rocky pier.

"It's so peaceful," I whispered.

"Yup," he agreed.

"I love quiet."

"Me too."

He seemed to appreciate the same things that I did. As we walked down the pier back towards shore, he turned around and kissed me. I was surprised.

"You don't like kissing me?" he asked.

"No," I lied, " I just...wasn't expecting it," actually *no, I didn't like kissing you.*

"You weren't expecting it? I would think you woulda thought I was gay if I didn't at least try."

I let him kiss me again, but this time I kissed him back. It was not his kiss but his vibes that pulled me in. Though I wanted him to keep his distance, I got a rush from being close to him --- something I had not experienced in years.

We kissed more that night, the chemistry was undeniable. I knew he wanted more and although it was pretty tempting, I had promised myself that I would never put myself in that situation again. I needed to know that the person would be there the next morning, I needed some sort of commitment, some sort of surety of intentions. I could not just *sleep* with someone. I wanted to *be* with someone.

Soon my cousin and I drove back to her apartment to rest. It was so late in the morning that the horizon began to glow with light. On our drive back, my phone rang. It was him calling me.

"I just wanted to say goodnight," he said.

The gesture was very saccharine and although I appreciated it, I could not help but wonder if my heart would go through the blender again. My gut told me that it was something real. That whole night, I could not look away from him and part of me knew that he felt it, too.

The next day, I barely heard from him. He texted me a few times, but the last text I sent him went unanswered. We were out very late the night before. *Maybe he was sleeping?* Had this feeling of love for him deceived me? I knew it was early on, but I believed in fairy tales, in love at first sight. Would he call me again?

My stomach sank as things began to look bleak. Over the next few days, I heard from him very sparingly. Still, my feelings for him continued to grow stronger. I knew I might get hurt, but this time I was prepared to take a chance.

Love was like skating onto thin ice --- you step out onto its surface knowing that there is a risk: that if it breaks you may drown. Hopeful that the ice is strong, you step on it anyway deciding to take your chances.

The energy you get from skating around and around on a frozen lake is indescribable. Nothing compares to the feeling you get when your skates cut through the fresh surface that first time.

I did not know if this new feeling would last, but I held onto it with the tenacity of a shark's bite. I liked him and I had not liked anyone in a while. When I was with the last few guys I dated, I felt empty inside. I wondered if I would ever meet someone I actually had feelings for, someone who would have feelings for me as well. I wondered if true love existed or if it was only reserved for a lucky few. From my perspective, it often seemed that way.

I had been in relationships where I was called names and sometimes physically injured, but they still felt safe. Safe in the sense that no one would ever take my heart and soul and bludgeon it to death *again* because I would not give anyone another chance to do that.

Inevitably, I learned that even with men I originally perceived to be *safe*, there were consequences. When they called me names like cunt, bitch, and whore, it stung for days but did not compare to the pain of finding true love, then having someone take it away.

He invited me back down to the shore for the 4th of July. My heart pounded as I drove down I-95 and then through the winding maze of houses that made up his neighborhood. When I walked in, he did not hug me. *That's not good.*

It was a gorgeous day, but he wanted to watch TV. I had no interest in drinking, still he got me a beer and insisted on sharing his strawberry daiquiri with me. After an hour of sitting on his couch, he still had not kissed me.

The sun began to go down.

"Let's go for a walk before the sun sets!"

He murmured at my suggestion then stood up. We walked down the street. The oversized beach houses blocked the view and caused us to miss the majority of the sunset. It was not until we reached the sand that we saw heavenly clouds of pastel pinks and blues floating across the sky. We took off our sandals and dangled our feet off the edge of the pier. The water rippled in shades of pastel pinks and blues; reflections from the sky.

"It's so pretty," I said, pointing down, "The way the clouds make the water look pink and blue."

He nodded, "It's constantly moving too, the water. Maybe you could use that in your book?"

He was right, the ocean was constantly moving; constantly changing.

We sat on the pier staring at the pastel-colored waves in silence. Suddenly, I remembered something. On the day we had met, I saw a lone swan in one of the inlets. I started to feel sad.

"What's wrong?" he asked.

I was surprised that he even noticed my mood change.

"Oh, nothing," I said, looking down.

"What?"

"Nothing. It's sad. You don't want to know, trust me."

"No, tell me!" He insisted.

"Are you sure?"

"Of course."

"Well, on the day we met, when I was driving to the shore, I saw a lone swan."

"So."

He looked puzzled.

"Don't you know about swans?" I asked.

"Not really."

"That they mate for life."

"So?" he still did not seem to get it.

"Well, it was all alone. That means that its mate must've died."

Soon the sun disappeared completely and the rainbow of clouds faded and turned the sky a dark blue. We could see 360 degrees of fireworks from where we sat on the long pier. So far from the beach, it felt like we were floating together in the middle of the sea. Behind us, fireworks shot off the beach as drunken men lit the gunpowder wicks in between taking drags off their cigars.

To our left, we saw various firework displays coming from the town which seemed so far away. Even on the horizon, fireworks from faraway cruise ships shot into the sky like Cupid's arrows.

"Look," he said, pointing them out to me.

Physically, he kept his distance and I wondered why.

The glow from each rocket illuminated our faces as we walked back towards the beach. It was now very dark. Back on shore, we sat in the sand and I dug my toes into the ground.

When the fireworks ended, we went back to his house. We sat on the couch and cuddled as we watched TV. Finally, he kissed me. I pulled away from him and gazed into his eyes.

"I've been waiting for you to do that all night."

I slept over his house that night. We held hands as we slumbered.

During the following week, he called one day after work and said he would come to my house and pick me up in his new corvette. I got dressed and waited, but he never showed up.

Shortly thereafter, the phone rang, "I'm sorry babe. I had to work late."

It was an hour drive to my house so I could see where he was coming from. That did not stop me from being disappointed and even more disappointed that it was now Thursday and he had not bothered to make weekend plans with me.

I spent Friday staring at my phone. It felt like middle school all over again. I tried to make plans with my friends --- anyone --- just to get my mind off him, but everyone already had plans. Inevitably I texted him, "Do you want to meet up?"

"Come over," he said.

He expected me to drive to come see him, again?

"Only if we can go somewhere," I countered.

When I arrived at his house he was sloppily drunk. I could not gauge just how drunk he was, but knew that he was not anywhere near sober. I was disappointed. *Maybe I should drive back to my house.* I thought about it, but it would be another hour long ride and I really liked him.

"You're wicked hot!" he said as I walked in the door.

"Thanks, but this is me barely trying," I smiled.

"You didn't even try to look good for me?"

We laughed.

We went to a local tiki bar where he ran into some guys he knew from high school. He ignored me to talk to them and did not bother to introduce me. The guys, though his age, were all married and there with their wives. They rolled their eyes at him when he turned his back and kept redirecting him towards me, *his date*. It was barely audible, but before we had left his house to go to the bar, I think I heard him tell his roommates that the only reason he was going out was because "I told her I'd take her somewhere if she came over."

"Did you get a drink yet?" he asked me.

"No. I was waiting for you."

"Well, why didn't you get one when I bought these guys a round?" he said pointing towards his high school friends.

"What are you talking about? You didn't buy them a round."

"Yeah, I did, I bought everyone drinks."

He walked off again, and I started a conversation with one of his friend's wives.

"He says he bought all of you drinks, but I'm pretty positive that he didn't since I've been standing here the whole time. Did he?"

She looked at me like I was crazy.

"No, he definitely did not."

"He must be really drunk." I said quietly to myself as I drifted off to a lone bar stool. He sat down beside me. I ordered a $2 beer. He ordered a rum and coke. When the bartender asked for $7 he put his hand in his pocket and then the other pocket and pulled out nothing. Now I was not only annoyed, but embarrassed.

"Don't you have money?" he asked me.

This was the same guy who had told me big stories about his Corvettes and Cadillacs.

"Don't *you* have money?"

"Here's a five," he said slapping it onto the bar, "you're gonna have to cover the rest."

I had yet to see any of those nice cars and soon found out that the beach house was not actually his, but his father's.

"Are you joking?" I demanded. " I don't have any cash."

I glared at him.

"Are you really asking me right now to put $2 on my debit card?"

The bartender witnessing this display politely told me not to worry about it and walked away.

Sometimes you skate out too far before you realize what you have done. It is not until then that you begin to hear the unmistakable sound of ice cracking. Your eyes widen. Nervously you lunge back towards land, but it is too late. You claw for the surface; claw for some sort of remnant of surface, something even vaguely resembling a surface, you just need something --- anything --- something solid to hold on to.

We went back to his apartment and hung out with his roommates. The place was littered with empty $50 sake bottles, the kind he liked to drink. I was having fun conversing with the other guys, but still contemplated leaving. I dreaded the long drive home, but had to make a decision before it got too late. We sat on the couch.

"Do you even like me?" I asked staring at him, my eyes piercing his.

"Of course I like you, *I love you*!"

Whoa. Not the response I expected.

"You love me!" I said, and he left the room embarrassed and went to the next room. "I knew it!" I said following him.

It was truly pathetic, the way I lit up after hearing *those three words.* Regardless of the night's events, I felt something for him and I was convinced that he felt it too.

"You love me," I teased him.

"Stop it," he said smirking.

"You love me," I taunted.

He got up and walked away.

"I'm just joking," I said motioning for him to come back, "If you like me so much how come you don't ever call or text me?"

"I'm...shy."

"Yeah, right."

"Uh huh."

"You must *really* like me then."

"I do," he replied.

"So you ignore me because you *really like me.* Does that make sense?"

I looked to one of his roommates.

"Do you ignore girls when you really like them?"

"Sometimes," his friend answered.

He sat back down on the couch beside me.

"I love you, too," I whispered into his ear.

We soon left and went to his part of the apartment, a loft on the top floor surrounded by trees. It seemed to float in the middle of the woods, it was so beautiful and peaceful. He kissed me and tried to go farther. I pushed him away.

"I'm just going to go home."

"No, no, sleep over."

"No that's okay, I'm just going to go."

"It's such a long drive home for you. Sleep over, we'll cuddle. It will be nice, but I'm going to warn you, I sleep naked."

We were deep in the woods with a gorgeous view of the forest. Cool summer breeze and the fresh scent of pine gently wafted into the bedroom as I lay wide awake. I turned in his direction and draped my arm over his back. His skin was baby soft.

"Do you really love me?" I asked.

I did not just need an answer, *I needed his love*. I did not just need his love, *I was counting on it*. It was the adrenaline I needed to keep my heart pumping. *Yes,* he was a total asshole, but I did not care. I had a heart! I had feelings! I was no Grinch, no Scarlett O'Hara, not even the Scarecrow from *The Wizard of Oz*. I did not just need any answer, I needed a *yes*. In fact, my life depended on it. He was my defibrillator and I was DOA.

"Yeah, hun," he said.

"I love you too," I smiled and fell into a happy slumber, still worried that maybe he did not.

The next morning, he disappeared to hang out with his roommate. Though he promised that he would take me out to breakfast, he suddenly had to go help his brother move.

"I'll try to stop over later," he said.

When later came, I did not hear from him. I texted him. He texted me back.

"Hey hun, sorry. Can't come over. My friend was in a car accident."

I called him immediately half wanting to console him, half wanting to see if he was lying, but he did not bother to answer the phone.

Days passed. I had not heard from him... *not so much as a text.*

One afternoon, I took my sick aunt to her doctor's appointment. The phone rang as we walked out of the office trying to dodge cold rain as we moved towards the car. I questioned his interest in me.

"I like you," he assured me. "I'm into you," he repeated, "but I have to go I'm bringing the truck back to the firehouse. I have a few more things to do before I finish up. I will call you back later."

Later came and he did not call, so I called him out of frustration. He said he had to go, but he would call me back in 15 minutes. Fifteen minutes passed, but he did not call. Soon I got frustrated and text-bombed him to the point of seething regret.

I was crushed. He had thrown around the word so loosely. *Love.* The word, the verb, the noun proved once again to mean nothing, to have no place in my life. I knew guys said stuff like that to get laid. I knew the two of us pairing up was for some reason unlikely, based solely on statistics: none of my other relationships had ever worked out. I hoped against everything that maybe just maybe it would work out and that maybe he really did love me. I had feelings for him after not having feelings for anyone in almost a decade. Now I was alone and not only mourning the loss of him, but also of the my previous boyfriend whom I had never fully gotten over.

Your clumsy attempt to cheat fate, to make it back to land before falling through is thwarted. And there you go plunging to your icy death. The cold water mercilessly punches you in the face. It is dark. You're confused. Your thoughts freeze. You have no thoughts. You cannot think. What happened?

For a few days, I waited and hoped he would get back to me. A friend invited me to go New Haven for lunch. On our drive home, I saw two swans silently gliding down a stream side-by-side. I still hoped he would call me back. After another week passed and I had not heard from him, I finally gave up and deleted him from my Facebook.

Was I so naïve? Why did I stay in this unhealthy situation and all the other ones? It was like I spent the whole day at the beach, but refused to get up when the tide came in. I knew I might drown. It was a risk I was willing to take because I did not feel like getting up. How could I stay with him even after seeing the amount of alcohol he carelessly drank regardless of the fact that I was there? Before I even showed up! I was desperately in need of love. *Desperately.*

I was alone again. I still had no one to collect sea glass with. I was terrified about my test results, but at least now I knew one thing : my ex boyfriend was wrong; my cold heartedness was not universal, rather, the result of being with *him.*

IV

Thessalonike

*Any other answer would send her into a violent fit aimed at sending the ship and
every sailor on board to the bottom of the sea-*

When I was a child, I pretended to be a mermaid. In the bath, I would twist my legs together like a fin and flap it around the water thumping it up against the fiberglass basin. Once a girl, now a mermaid. Every little girl wants to be a mermaid; the half fish half woman, who throws herself into the sea to rescue drowning sailors; the men overboard.

I threw myself after several. Surely this behavior could not have been influenced by *Splash,* a movie I watched incessantly as a child. In the movie, Daryl Hannah plays a mermaid who saves Tom Hanks' overboard character from drowning on more than one occasion.

I threw myself into my last relationship as if I was trying to save his life. The way he behaved towards me when we were alone was very confusing --- it differed so much from the way he treated me in public. For a long time I was not entirely certain that I was being abused. He was so nice to *everyone else*. He needed my help. For some reason he was so down on himself and for some reason I saw something great in him, something he did not see, something he could not see because it was something that never truly existed.

He was not the only one I tried to save. The musician, claimed he was not an alcoholic and that his near nightly binge-drinking was something that "everyone did in college." *Not to that degree.* He had once entrapped me in my dorm room when he was wasted. I was terrified, but easily got out; he backed down no problem.

The last night we were in my dorm room together was different. He drank a six pack in less than an hour, downing one after another like a cartoon character's drink disappears with such unbelievable ease. After he finished the beer, he said he was going to my neighbors to play video games. They had rigged a projector to their system and were playing video games across the entire wall of our dorm's common room. I sat in my room alone reading, but after ten minutes of reading my book, I decided that it looked like they were having fun and I wanted to play, too.

When I got there he was gone, in fact, he had never even swung by at all. It was not until a few hours later he came back into the dorm stumbling drunk. Later that night, he got kicked out of the dorms permanently when my Residential Advisor saw him take a swing at me.

There was another incident the previous year. We got into an argument over the phone and as a result, he showed up at my dorm drunk. I refused to see him. He called me begging and crying. I often ended up caving in and talking to him as I did on this night because there were many nights, *many of the nights I have already mentioned,* in which he threatened me and said he would commit suicide.

In hindsight, I should have just ignored his bullshit pleas. That night, I crept down the cold dorm stairwell. Outside pale yellow, orange and pink long stem roses were strewn across the entrance of my dorm, in the hedges, and on the ground. Clearly he was upset.

"Hayl!" he yelled jumping out at me from behind a bush.

I screamed, startled by him. His eyes shined wildly like a wolf's in moonlight. It was freezing out and he only wore only a t-shirt, his arms crossed over his chest. This was typical attire for him along with his usual claim that he "wasn't cold." He was not only a terrible alcoholic, but a martyr; he did things to hurt himself just so he could refuse any help that was offered.

Then there was my first boyfriend, the one I was in love with. He too would go out drinking and come home totally shit-faced and call me names. On several occasions, he came home completely trashed; white as a sheet. One inevitable argument that ensued caused him to try to jump out of our first story window. It was not until after we broke up and I was watching *Goodfelllas* that I realized what was going on. Ray Liota's character was getting high on coke. I finally recognized the odd look my boyfriend had come home with. At the time I had no idea what was going on.

I closed my eyes and let the hot water pour over me. While the water slowly began to soothe my aching muscles, I noticed that the entire house was very quiet. This stillness magnified my sense of aloneness. If someone were to break in, I would be rendered helpless if overpowered by the intruder. And what if I had a seizure while taking a bath? Who would save me from drowning? And what about eating? What if I was eating a piece of dry bread and it got lodged in my throat? What could I do if I started to choke?

I was so alone, *so alone.* Never before had I minded being alone, but I did not just feel alone. I felt hollow like a seashell; something had been taken; something was gone, and I had no idea what it was. Something was missing, taken in stealth, and I was clueless, still.

Alone I went to the gynecological exam, to see if the ASCUS, atypical cells of unknown significance, reading on my test was just a fluke or if maybe something was really wrong with my cervix. I was relieved to leave the chilly office and hopeful that the results would turn out okay.

During the entire summer we spent together in Rhode Island, we did not go to Block Island once. *Not once.* In fact, the closest I had ever been to Block Island was the beach in Rhode Island. I remember the first time I noticed the land mass across the way.

Blinded by the sun, we loomed in the sand draped over our soggy beach towels. That weekend, my boyfriend's entire family had come up to stay at the beach house. He and his grandfather passed a crossword puzzle back and fourth taking turns at trying to solve it. It was stuff like that that made me feel like I was dating an 80-year-old man. I could not help but be disgusted.

Sitting up, I tried to pretend that my boyfriend was not working on a crossword puzzle with his grandfather. I looked forward towards the horizon and kept my mouth shut. Brushing the sticky sand off of my skin, I cupped my hand over my brow shielding my eyes from the sun. I looked outwards: the dark blue water, so calm and methodical. *What was that?* I wondered.

From some of the Connecticut beaches, you could see the Manhattan Skyline. It stood clearly clearly silhouetted in the west; a picturesque postcard. This definitely was not Manhattan.

"What is that? Is that...Block Island?"

Briefly he looked up from his crossword to address my statement.

"Yeah, probably."

"I've never been. We should go sometime."

"Uh huh," he turned his head back down towards his crossword.

I had tried to do the crossword puzzles with him before. I tried to pretend it did not bother me: that he and I were in on a Friday night doing crossword puzzles with his grandmother. But he would often pull it away from me, wanting to do it himself. I think my hard pencil lines annoyed him. They were difficult to erase. If he was unsure of the answer, he would carefully jot it in the margin, leaving the small crossword squares virgin and pristine.

"Well, maybe next summer?" I said.

He looked up at me and nodded. It seemed that he had willingly agreed to go with me. Going to Block Island had to wait until the next summer because this summer he endlessly complained of money troubles. If I dared to press the issue, he would most certainly shame me for being so selfish when I knew he was behind on his bills. I was happy at the prospect though, that he would go with me to Block Island the following summer. At the time, I viewed this sand-castle-in-the-sky agreement as thoughtful. It was thoughtful that he was taking my desires into consideration and even better that he genuinely seemed interested in going to Block.

By that time next year, we were broken up and I spent the summer dating one guy after another. By the time I was on my second or third guy, I no longer missed him. I was over him, yet with every new dating disappointment I was sad and now had a new person to get over. Like a person who forever chases their hangovers with booze, eventually a morning comes when a break from drinking is needed and on that morning, you have to deal with the hangover.

I thought about the day I drove down to Niantic; the day I met the fireman, my *latest hang-up*. Alone, a lone swan swam in one of the river's inlets. A lonely life it must lead: awaiting nothing but death. Does one ever get used to being lonely? With each subsequent break-up or failed relationship, does the emotional load become easier to bear? I did not have any evidence to support that statement, in fact, it seemed to get worse.

I still had not heard from him. Though I deleted him from Facebook, a part of me hoped he would call me back, even after I text-bombed him. Though he was a complete drunken idiot that night, he still affected me profoundly. Before we went to sleep, he played his drum set. One of the songs he played was by the band Korn. When I was in high school, I loved Korn, but then I started dating my first boyfriend and he did not like my Hot Topic style. He wanted an Abercrombie girl, and I complied the best I could. That was the first piece of myself I gave away to a man who did not care; a man who would never appreciate or understand who I was.

It was the same with my Rhode Island boyfriend, the psychopath. He did his best still, I was not an Abercrombie girl: he did not want that. He wanted someone unnoticeable. He was one of those guys who "takes a beautiful girl and hides her away from the rest of the world." I never conformed to his standards, but his comments about my attire still made me feel bad. He wanted me hidden in plain sight. So when I heard "Blind," by Korn, a part of me that I thought had died was resurrected. I still liked the music, though for years I told myself I did not because it did not fit the image of the girl my boyfriends wanted me to portray.

I was depressed. I felt *dowdy*. I spent my time thinking about the sea and its elements. The connection I felt to the ocean was stronger than ever, as if the moon pulled me inward along with the tides. I had not seen it in years, but suddenly I became preoccupied with the movie *Splash*, a movie in which Daryl Hannah plays a mermaid who falls in love with Tom Hanks, a mortal.

Perhaps it was my childhood memory trying to sooth me during my time of heartbreak, regardless I could not find a copy of the video or DVD anywhere. The long hair, goddess look and femininity of Madison, Daryl Hannah's mermaid character, felt completely the opposite of me. She was magical and romantic and I was frumpy. She was colorful and I was gray.

I decided to get my hair braided. There was something sensual about long braided hair. Something exotic. And it was summertime. I had not felt anything but frumpy since the time I began dating my ex and I wanted to feel vibrant again. I wanted to feel alive. I took some money out of the ATM and drove to an African hair-braiding salon in the city.

That night, two West African women worked tirelessly over my head. They spoke to each other in French and answered their phones in broken English. I tried to understand what they were saying but only occasional words were recognizable words pop out, like *"les enfants," the children,* and various days of the week.

Four hours later, long braids trailed down my neck and dangled over the small of my back. I had been transformed into a goddess. I felt good again. From then on, I could not walk down the street without men and women turning around to look at me as I passed. Somehow I had recaptured this feminine beauty, this power I thought I lost, a sensuality I had been missing for so long. I felt like a mermaid. If I undid the braids it would easily capture the long crimped beach blown style of Daryl Hannah's mermaid locks.

My wild braids brought back the spirit I had been missing. Somehow he had drained me of my confidence, femininity and beauty. Had he seen me now, had we still been dating, he would have been mortified to be seen with me in public. I laughed at the thought of him.

About halfway through the relationship I was hooked on him and the dynamics shifted fiercely and rapidly like a boat before it capsizes and like a dutiful captain, I went down with the ship. Somehow I became the one who did all the pursuing. In the beginning, he came to my side in my time of weakness offering to help. I became the one trying to fix his life; trying to save him from himself. It was not the first time I became the savior unwittingly. Unfortunately, when I moved on to a new man the old pattern continued.

Now weeks after this new relationship ended, I was the victim of a broken heart again. *He said he loved me.* It was a short two week fling in which I ended up exactly where I began, but worse. *He said he had not felt that way about anyone in years.* Perhaps he was not the first one to whisper this false testament of love into my ear.

It was much like Alexander the Great's sister, Thessalonike, who turned into a mermaid after Alexander died.

She stopped ships as they passed through the Aegean to ask the sailors, "Is King Alexander Alive?"

Despite the truth, she would only tolerate one answer, "Yes, he lives and reigns and conquers the world."

Upon hearing that she would calm the sea so the sailors could safely pass, but if a sailor told her the truth, it was another story. Suddenly there was a strong gale. Huge tidal waves crashed onto the ship, her will ultimately put the sailor's lives in danger. Is that why men told me they loved me? Did they fear my wrath otherwise?

It was Thessalonike's hair that made her a mermaid. Wrought with grief when Alexander died, she threw herself to her own death off a cliff and unto the sea. But she did not die, *she could not.* Years earlier, Alexander had bathed her hair in aqua from the Flask of Immortal Water which he retrieved on his quest for The Fountain of Immortality.

How foolish was I to think that he loved me just because he said he did. The sea stayed calm for him until his actions proved his words otherwise. Still, I had not mastered the lesson that words did not mean a thing. He was afraid to tell me the truth, afraid that if he did he might drown in a turbulent emotional tempest. He did not love me. He did not even like me. Alexander is dead!

Soon I met another man, an educator. He was down to earth and a special education teacher who seemed nice. I was not entirely attracted to him at first, he was brawny and bald. His sense of fashion was not the best and he always wore a necklace made of brown leather. After two dates his interest seemed to dwindle, he called me less and could not make plans with me, especially not on the weekends because of the various softball leagues he participated in.

But about a week into dating, he invited me to go to a beach party with him on Block Island on a Saturday. I was a bit nervous about going with him, we had not even kissed. But I was excited about Block Island. Though I had lived in New England most of my life, I had never visited it.

The previous summer, I took a trip to Florida with my ex. On one particularly sweltering day, we pulled over on the side of the road at Ormond Beach. The ocean was warm bathwater, a sharp contrast to the rigid New England shoreline. I threw myself into the sea and let the soft waves roll over me. I came up for air. Wet hair slid down my back the way it does when a graceful mermaid surfaces in the films. I knew nothing but the moment, the feeling of the warm water dripping from my hair and back and into the sea.

"Did you see that?" He said interrupting my thoughts and pointing outwards.

"Huh?" I said startled.

"I think I saw a fin maybe a whale or something."

It surfaced again then disappeared back into the sea. The pattern continued. I was scared. Was it a shark? Suddenly I realized what it was. It was a dolphin! I had finally seen one!

On the drive down to Florida from Connecticut, I shared my plan with him.

"I want to go on a boat tour to see the wild dolphins."

"Well, have fun. I'm not going to waste my money to go with you to see *dolphins*."

His words crushed me a little, always so nasty. Why was he always so obstinate?

"That's fine," I said, "I will go without you. You can wait for me on the pier."

"*Well, then maybe I'll go,*" he said.

He, of course, ended up going with me. He was the only person on the boat who sat quietly unimpressed as pods of beautiful dolphins gracefully swam by our small boat. I was the happiest I had been in a long time. One dolphin even swam by with her little baby. Like people, they traveled together in families.

I was really looking forward to going to Block Island with the new guy. I started to like him more and more everyday. In my mind, I pictured how the afternoon would play out as we toured the island on scooters. It had been a romantic day on Block, but now the sun was going down. Soon, we would have to catch the ferry back to New London. We pulled our scooters over at a bluff as the colorful rays streaked across the sky, providing the perfect backdrop for our first kiss.

He became even more distant the week before our outing. A few days before the trip, he sent me a sly text saying that because of rain his softball game had been canceled and rescheduled for Saturday. He did not specify which Saturday, nor did he mention anything about no longer being able to go to Block Island with me.

"You mean *this* Saturday?" I asked.

"Yes."

"So we're not going to Block Island?" I texted him.

"Right," he said.

"That sucks. I was really looking forward to it."

"Block Island will always be there and can go some other time this summer."

The way his pronouns suddenly vanished from his vocabulary sounded pretty non-committal to me. Damn texting.

So no more beach party on Block Island for me that Saturday. I was beyond bummed and over the next few days his texting slowed until it came to a complete halt.

I was pretty disappointed. I redirected my focus to once again trying to obtain a copy of *Splash*. I still had not found one. It was so unpopular that they did not sell it on DVD. Finally, my father surprised me with a copy that he had found at the local library. It was probably as old as the movie itself, a tattered VHS tape.

S*plash* begins when a young boy, who is touring Cape Cod with his family, falls off of a boat and into the Cape. A little girl mermaid comes to his rescue. After she saves him from drowning, she helps him back to the boat. By chance they reunite in adulthood when he becomes stranded on a boat off the coast of Cape Cod and consequently falls out of it almost drowning again. After rescuing him, she leaves him on the shore and runs away, he chases after her begging merely to know her name.

She swims away, but later tracks him down after she realizes that he has left his wallet behind. She goes to a sunken ship and looks at an old map where she figures out how to navigate her way from Cape Cod to New York. Days later, she shows up on Liberty Island completely naked looking for him.

I barely heard from him, until Saturday night. That night he texted me furiously. I was excited at first; he had not texted me that much since we first started talking. He told me that they lost the game, which had been rescheduled to a field in New London. New London? *That's weird.* New London was the same town where we were suppose to catch the ferry *to go to Block Island.*

Later that evening, he texted me saying that they were at a bar in Mystic. This made me super suspicious. I Googled his softball league. It was not that I was a stalker; it *was* that I did not want to continue dating a liar. Online I found no cancellations for the night in question and certainly no games rescheduled in New London. From what I learned, only middle school softball leagues played on their fields.

I checked his Facebook. He had two new friends: girls from New York. *Hmm, I wonder if they were at the New London game, too?* Sarcasm.

One of the girls wrote a comment on his wall, something about barnacles... *that was weird.* Anyone would have thought I was crazy for being so suspicious. *Actually a few people did think I was crazy,* but it was really grating me. I started to feel like the biggest loser in the world, realizing now that he was probably texting me more out of guilt than interest. It was all too coincidental and I did not believe in coincidences.

That night, one of his two new Facebook friends changed her profile picture to a shot of her and the other girl at a beach party. It was a gorgeous sunny day much like that Saturday afternoon, the afternoon I was suppose to be with him on Block Island. In the background of this picture, the camera had captured a man who just happened to be passing by, a man who also happened to have a shiny bald head and the same type of necklace that the guy I was dating always wore. I still wanted to give him the benefit of the doubt.

In addition to flaking on me, he now claimed that he was busy every night of the week with his softball games, but could perhaps hang out with me after he got out of work the next night, a Sunday night. He said he would let me know. By the time he got around to texting me that day, it was 9 at night.

I was so annoyed with him that I had already deleted him from Facebook. Now I was furious. The other girl had put the same picture up as her Facebook profile picture, but this time, I was able to click on and enlarge it. Now there was no doubt in my mind that it was him in the background of the beach party photo. It was very difficult for me at this point to be mature; to act like an adult.

"Hey, I can meet up in a half hour, but it's Sunday, so I don't think anywhere will be open too late," his text read.

I was so tempted to make plans with him and stand him up. I was so hurt by his mistreatment of me and sad that I still did not get to visit Block Island. Without blinking, I sighed and texted back.

"I cant make it, good luck with everything."

At the end of the Florida trip with my ex, we stopped at a beach in Naples. I took my sandals off and after a few steps into the water, looked down and saw the most beautiful shell; a perfectly svelte spiral. It was what I had been looking for my entire life, but I had never found one completely intact. It would look beautiful among my collection of beach treasures: sea glass, stones, and scalloped shells. I plucked it out of the water.

As I was admiring my new shell, it began to spit water at me. I was puzzled at first but then I flipped it over and saw that a black mollusk was living inside.

It spit at me again, this time in my face. At first I was annoyed, but then impressed by the small mollusk's tenacity. The gall of the mollusk when faced with a giant like myself was nothing less than admirable.

"I like your attitude," I said before apologizing to it and placing it back into the Gulf exactly where I'd found it.

I thought back to a gift shop in Daytona that we stopped earlier in the week. Its shelves were lined with conch and various spiral shells that looked a lot like this one. At the time, I imagined that the shells on the shelves had been collected from the beach early in the morning by one of the clerks after the animals inside had died and consequently washed ashore, but now I wasn't so sure. Had they knowingly taken these beautiful creatures out of the ocean and killed the animals inside in order to make a quick five bucks off of their shells? I think so.

Now twice dumped in a month's time, I felt blindsided. Had I no judgment? I was still hung up on the man I had met earlier that summer at the ocean in Niantic. How could love feel so real, yet be so fake? I was terrified, if I could not trust myself, who could I trust? And then my ex, the one who almost murdered me was on my mind again. The thought of him gave me chills. His rage was alarming; the amount of hatred he directed at me for no reason. I never hated anyone in my life until now.

My aunt wanted to know why I went out with men who treated me so badly. Why I allowed myself to be treated this way and why I stayed so long in these relationships? Though she demanded to know these things, the rest of my family and friends looked on in silence. Did they know something I did not? Perhaps they viewed me as a lost cause. Was I?

The more she criticized the men I dated, the more I disagreed with her in my head. For one, she did not understand the dynamics of any of my relationships and even went as far to call me "stupid" for staying with these men for so long. *That hurt.* I was not stupid, *I was vulnerable.*

People wondered how I could put up with these men and stay with them after some of the awful things they said and did to me. From my perspective and some of the things that I had been through earlier in my life, what they said and did to me did not always seem so bad. Even after everything that happened throughout these relationships, the most abusive relationship I ever had was the relationship I had with myself.

A month later, I met another guy and fell for him hard. I was still hurt by what happened with the other guys earlier in the summer, but open to giving this guy a chance though he was a bit older than me: like 20 years older than me. That was not what made me want to date him entirely. Mainly, I was impressed by his persistence as he started off our friendship by contacting me relentlessly until I finally agreed to go on a date with him.

He was a bartender who worked at a bar in Old Saybrook on the weekends and spent the rest of the week in the home he owned on Block Island. He came from a very affluent family and was the last of eight children. What I really loved about him was the fact that he was Irish and always wore a family heirloom, his great grandfather's wedding ring. It was a thick silver ring encircled with a Celtic knot.

I had always had a thing for Irish guys especially since my travels to the country. Ireland was beautiful, one big island, green and lush. I easily fell in love with the quaint cottages that dotted the island's landscape. Even the cemeteries were gorgeous each headstone crowned with an ornate Celtic cross. As we drove up the Western coast, the mist gave the country a mystical feeling. It was the perfect setting for any love story to begin.

I had seen a profile of him on a dating website, and although he was handsome, because he was so much older than me, I did not think twice about him. Add to that the fact that he was a bartender. I did not date bartenders; they were usually serial players. I forgot all about him until one day he contacted me, messaged me and begged me to go on a date with him. He said that he wanted to take me some place romantic.

"No thanks," I said without guilt.

In my mind there was nothing romantic about a first date. It was more of a meeting with the sole purpose of deciding whether or not you were attracted enough to the person to go on a second date. He was kind of an ass. He told me that at 25, I was the oldest person he ever dated.

"Ditto," I replied.

Apparently he was used to dating 18-year-olds and considered those in their mid-twenties to be aged.

He had been overtly sexual from the beginning, and I had no interest in giving *it* up, least of all not *that* fast. I found him amusing anyway; our banter and flirtation was fun, he would try and I would promptly shoot him down, then he would come back for more. Despite not getting what he wanted, he seemed to like me and we got along well. Until we got into a disagreement and I deleted him from Facebook. Then I did not hear from him for over a week, until my birthday.

I was not having the best birthday. I was a little down and thinking about the year's relationship failures when my phone rang. It was him. I stared at it for a minute and let it go to voice mail. I did like him and was attracted to him, but hewas not very nice to me.

Finally, a text came in from him, "What the hell is your problem?"

"Excuse me?" I wrote back, "Oh, I get it. That must be a typo and what you meant to write was 'Happy Birthday.'"

There was a long pause before he responded.

"I'm sorry. I didn't mean to be rude. I'm just upset because my friend died."

Ha, I scoffed. I had heard about more car accidents, illnesses, sudden narcolepsy, and run-ins with the police from these guys than I could bear and now he expected me to believe that his friend died? No one ever used that one on me before. I completely ignored his statement.

"Come over," he persisted.

"Excuse me?"

"Come over. I need someone to console me."

"Right. It's my birthday, you can come over here," we lived over an hour apart.

"I can't. I have to work at the bar tonight."

"Oh well," I wrote, "Ahem, *Happy Birthday, Hayley.*"

"Happy Birthday," he finally texted me. "Come on, come over. I have your birthday present waiting for you right here."

"Bullshit wait, what is it?"

"I can't tell you."

"I knew you didn't get me anything. You didn't even remember it was my birthday."

"I'll give you a clue. You can wear it."

"Unless it's jewelry, I don't want it."

Later that night, I received a friend request from him on Facebook. I debated whether or not I should re-add him, but inevitably did. After adding him, I went to his wall and was shocked to read his Facebook status, "And my condolences to the Kensen family." Several other people responded to his comment and added their condolences. He was not lying.

The next day, we started texting again. I felt a little guilty for not believing him, but I reminded myself that I had plenty of reason not to. That afternoon, he said that he had to go to Mystic to run errands. I loved Mystic. He invited me to go with him. He said he had a few things to do and then we could grab lunch. Without thinking, I got in the car.

This would be our second date. We actually did go on a very nice first date before we abruptly stopped talking to one another and I consequently Facebook defriended him. After this very pleasant date, it was as if previously undisturbed rotting corpses had been unearthed from a shipwreck and began to surface one at a time.

Before our first date, we spent a few nights speaking online. One of the first things he told me about was his house on Block Island.

He then asked, "Do you like planes? Do you like flying?"

"I hate flying," I responded.

"Oh," he said. "Well would you mind if we took a small plane when we go to visit my house on Block?"

I thought about this for a minute and began to backtrack. *Well,* I suppose I would try anything *at least once.*

For the past year, it seemed as if I had been stuck on a raft between Block Island and the mainland and that every time I got close to a landing on the beaches of Block, a huge wave would crash into me and push me back towards the Rhode Island shore. At this point, I would have to begin my pathetic paddling towards the island all over again. Now I was about to land on Block via a private airplane with a man who had an actual residence there. A house! Suddenly all the other guys and their false promises of Block Island seemed insignificant in comparison. Block for a day? Block for an afternoon? How about Block for a lifetime? I pictured our future married life together, me and this sexy Irishman on Block where he ran his own fishing business and owned various boats.

He was a lifelong Rhode Islander, a sailor who had always lived on the water. I just loved the whole New England feel to his personality; his sharp Yankee accent made him sound just like a Kennedy.

Our first date started off okay. He asked me to meet him at a romantic restaurant on the river. It had some type of mill and a gorgeous view.

"No," I said.

First dates did not need to be romantic unless one person had ulterior motives. Instead I agreed to meet him at a Mexican restaurant halfway between our homes when it was still daylight. I pulled into the restaurant's empty parking lot. He was not there and the restaurant appeared to be closed.

I called him on my cell. It took a few tries for him to answer. When he finally picked up we quickly figured out that the restaurant was closed on Mondays. He invited me to meet him in a town farther up the interstate and closer to his place: Chester.

Chester was a stereotypically charming and small seaside New England village. It was old and surely colonial. Scenic stone buildings and homes surrounded the town's center. I had always wanted to go to the old Irish pub on the corner. It was beautiful and I pictured us sharing a plate on its veranda. Once before, I had stopped in Chester with my last boyfriend on a drive home from Rhode Island. That Sunday afternoon, the town was hosting a farmer's market.

From the beginning, my ex copped an attitude with me as we walked from stand to stand. I complained to him because he kept walking either farther ahead of me or way behind me. He retaliated against my innocent grievance by calling me a "fucking bitch." I had difficulty hiding the tears that began to stream down my face as we walked past the fruit and veggie vendors.

Without warning, he walked away from me and back to the car leaving me in the middle of an open bakery stand. I stood dumbfounded in between shelves that brimmed with artisan loaves of bread. On principle, I did not follow him, not immediately at least, but soon after found myself walking towards his car.

"Will you stop it?" I begged.

"Get in the fucking car! We're done! Just get in. I'm taking you home."

"What is your problem? Can you just stop it? Can't we just have a nice day? It's a fuckin' farmer's market for Christ's sake! Can't we just *not fight* for once? All I wanted was to buy some jam!"

"Get in the fuckin' car or I'm leaving you here."

Defeated I slumped down into the bucket seats of his hideous sports car, something only the whitest of white trash would drive. He took off at record speed winding down Chester's narrow streets, streets built hundreds of years ago for horse and buggies, not for Dale Earnhardt Jr. wannabes.

"Slow down!" I screamed. He drove faster.

"Stop the fuckin car!" I demanded. "Stop the car! Let me out!"

I protested until he pulled into the parking lot of a industrial complex. I got out, grabbed my clothes, my camping chair, and sat on the curb.

"What are you going to do?" he asked. I ignored him. "What are you going to do? *Just sit there?*"

It was a hot summer day. The sun scorched my face and blinded me. Sweat started to dribble down my forehead as I sat on the curb waiting for him to go away and leave me alone.

"I'm going to call my father!" I screamed.

He took off and I dialed my dad begging him to pick me up.

"Are you serious?" My dad asked.

It was over an hour away, but I needed a ride. Soon my boyfriend drove

back and my father urged me to get back into the car with him. He did not feel like

picking me up and I did not feel like anyone loved me. With no expression on my

face I rode with him in the car until we got to my house and he dropped me off. I

got out of the car and wished I was dead.

I called him as I pulled onto the main street of Chester. I was less than a

block away from where my ex boyfriend had parked his car the day of the farmer's

market --- the parking lot where the fight escalated.

"I'm on my way," he said.

"Okay," I said, "Look for a black Sportage."

I idled at the curb until he walked up alongside my truck. I was shocked

by how thin he was; much thinner than in his pictures, so thin that he looked like a

junkie.

"Why don't you park your car where mine is and I'll drive to the

restaurant."

He got in my car and I immediately smelled alcohol on his breath.

"Were you drinking before you got here?"

"No, I had a drink at the pub while I was waiting for you."

"Just one?" I had to ask because the smell of alcohol was overpowering.

"A Manhattan."

"Oh."

I nervously parked my car next to his and got into the vehicle with him. It

was an old Mercedes with Maine license plates.

"Maine?"

"Yes, we have a house on the coast."

I was nervous as he pulled the car out of the lot, but luckily he did not drive too fast. Nervously, I reminded myself of what *they* say: that you can have at least two or three drinks and not be over the legal limit, *I'm sure he was fine.*

We tried to figure out where to dine, as the Mexican restaurant was still closed. I suggested the Irish pub on the corner.

"We can't go there," he said. "My ex-girlfriend's best friend works there and she hates me. "

That worried me a bit, but I soon dismissed this red flag because the evening went smoothly, delightfully well. We took off to Essex another small shoreline town with cute shops, narrow roads, and cobblestones.

We ended up at a posh upscale restaurant. Without reservations, we could not get a table and had to sit at the bar. That did not matter to me, what mattered was that he was very polite and courteous. I was impressed that he remembered that I was a vegetarian and ordered accordingly. He even ordered my dinner for me and requested a vegetarian appetizer without my prompting. At times, it was hard to believe that this was the same man who had been so overtly sexual in text and instant messages. It was hard to believe that this was the same man who had texted me a picture of his penis, *yes* his penis.

Next, we went to the bar where he worked. As we drove to the pub, he lit a cigarette, "Do you mind?" he asked.

"Actually, I almost died from pneumonia a few years ago and I'm not suppose to be around smoke."

He immediately dropped the entire cigarette out the driver's side window. My comment introduced the subject of almost dying into the conversation. He told me the story about the time he almost drowned.

"I was drinking all night, alone on one of my boats when a storm blew through. The waves became harsh and choppy. I fell overboard and into the water. As the rain pelted the ocean's surface I watched the boat drift farther and farther away from me. I treaded water and unsuccessfully tried to catch up to it. That's the last thing I remember. When the sun came up at dawn, I found myself laying sprawled out in my boat soaked in seawater."

Once we were at the bar, I said I knew how to read palms, but it was just an excuse for me to hold his hand. Afterwards, he disappeared into the back room and reappeared with Irish coffee, a plate of tiramisu, and two forks. It was sweet, two strangers sharing a dessert from one plate, very *Lady and the Trampish*.

The night continued to go well until the other people he worked with started bugging me to give them palm readings because they saw that I read his. He suggested that now was a good time to duck out and invited me to his apartment. His apartment happened to be conveniently located above the bar. I raised my eyebrows suspiciously.

"Don't worry," he said.

"I'm not worried. You promised you wouldn't try anything, so you better keep your word," I warned.

His apartment was very neat and well put together. He did not try anything, well, he did keep trying to cuddle with me. I caved fairly easily and lay my head across his hard chest as we continued to watch a movie.

He wore a silver necklace and pendant. I found both the necklace and the Celtic ring he wore to be extremely sexy; there was something hot about a man who wore carefully chosen jewelry.

"What is it? On this necklace?" I asked.

"It's Saint Christopher. My mother bought it for me."

"Why?"

"She's always worried about me," he said rolling his eyes. "It's suppose to protect me from an untimely death and violent accidents."

The movie ended. Nothing happened. He drove me back to my truck; it was one o'clock in the morning. Before I exited the car, he gave me the most innocent and soft kiss on the lips. I smiled.

"Goodnight," I said as he kissed me again lightly before I hopped back into my truck.

Things did not go so smoothly the next time we spoke. From the beginning, I told him that I was not looking for a sexual relationship, that I wanted to really get to know the person first, that I did not want to be hurt again.

He said he was fine with that, but then on Facebook Chat said, "If you're not going to have sex with me, you have to do something to pleasure me."

"What did you just say? *Pleasure* you?"

"Yes, *pleasure* me."

"Wow! It's all about you, huh?"

"You have to give me blow jobs or something," he became more demanding and increasingly vulgar.

An argument ensued. I was sad. I liked him. Then I gave up and went to sleep. The next day he invited me to his house.

When I was almost there, he texted me "You're going to blow me right?"

"*Wrong.*"

"Don't bother coming over. If you're not going to blow me I'm going to take a nap."

I was not about to turn around. I was almost there and a big hurricane was approaching. I knew I would not be able to come out that way to see him again anytime soon. I parked near his apartment. His car was there. I climbed the stairs and knocked on the door. No answer. I texted him. Nothing. I called him. No response.

More than a week passed and then I finally heard from him, on my birthday. In that week, he did not text me or anything. It was as if he fell off the face of the planet. Now I was driving down to see him again to go to Mystic for lunch.

"You're going to answer the door this time right?"

"I have no idea what you are talking about. I must've been sleeping."

"*Right.*"

I pulled up to his place and went to the door. I was emotionally handshy; a little bit nervous that he would stand me up again. Earlier I complained that he did not even mention that I looked pretty on our first date. I waited at the door. He finally opened it. He towered over me with a look of surprise on his face. His eyes were extremely glassy. He held the door open and motioned with his hands for me to come in.

"You look pretty," he said immediately. *Smart man.*

We sat on his futon as he rudely perused his Facebook while sipping a mango flavored alcoholic beverage from a can.

"I can't believe he's dead," he said as he clicked through the pictures of a guy who looked younger than myself. *Oh, that's what he was looking at.* A casualty of what appeared to be a drinking and driving accident one late night on Block.

I was anxious to have him all to myself, to go on some sort of date with him. Additionally, as each second passed and we still sat sitting at his computer, I became more and more annoyed with him. At this point, I did not really care that his friend died. I was no longer invested in him or any possible future, so I just shut my mouth and tried to be supportive, nodding at all the right times, and agreeing with his passing comments. He had been so unreliable that I no longer took anything about him seriously.

Finally he stood up, put on a pair of sunglasses, and grabbed his car keys. He held the door open for me and held the drink in his other hand. I eyed it. *Was he going to drink and drive?*

"Do you mind driving?" he asked.

"What? Why? Are you drunk?"

I was annoyed and confused. I had just driven an hour to get to his place.

"You can drive my car."

"No, that's okay, I'll drive mine."

"No take mine," he insisted pressing the keys of his Mercedes convertible into my hand.

It was an older sports model and it accelerated much faster than my Kia. On our entire drive down 95 towards Mystic, he talked about his friend who died *on the phone with his brother.* Though I felt rude interrupting because of the delicate nature of the subject matter, as the minutes passed, I became increasingly annoyed.

"So, I'm like your chauffeur or something?" I asked.

"No, hold on," he said something to his brother, then hung up the phone.

Now he was paying too much attention to me, to my driving.

"Why are you driving so fast?" He shouted.

"What? I'm going the speed limit!"

"No way, your driving fast. And do you have to hit *every* pothole in the road?"

Was he nuts? There weren't any potholes!

On our drive to his first stop, the bank, he casually mentioned that *maybe he did want a relationship after all.*

"Really?" I said and kissed him. "Take off your sunglasses so I can see your eyes."

He had nice blue eyes.

"Not now," he said.

On our way back towards Mystic, I started to question him a little.

"You really didn't hear me knocking at your door last week?"

"I told you not to come over, that I was going to be sleeping."

"And you were so nasty to me the last time we talked online --- so mean. You said you did a line that night or something?"

"Oh yeah. Sorry about that," he chuckled. "Ya, *I think I did a line that night.*"

"You did?" *Oh great.* "I thought you didn't like coke."

"I don't. Did I say it was coke?"

"I'm not sure, maybe you did."

"I don't think so. I don't do coke. It was heroine."

"Heroine." *What the fuck.* "You do heroine?"

"Just that once..."

"Are you crazy?"

"It was *just that once.*"

"Are you gonna do it again?"

"Well maybe. It felt *really* good."

"No shit. I can't date someone that does heroine, *seriously.*"

"It's not really that big of a deal...it's just that opiates have a bad reputation."

"Um. Yeah. Because their dangerous."

"Their not so bad."

"Heroine? N*ot so bad?*"

"It just has a bad connotation."

Really? I raised my eyebrows as he continued to ramble, "Opiates were legal for centuries in the States. They weren't banned until recent times. And in Asia everyone does them."

"We're not in Asia. *I can't go out with someone who does heroine,"* I mumbled to both myself and him.

"I only did it that once..."

"So you might not do it again?"

"But I really liked it."

We drove through downtown Mystic in silence. I parked on a side road. He cringed and jerked in anticipation and fear at the slightest turn of the wheel. We walked across the street to another Mexican restaurant, but it was closed.

We walked towards Main Street Mystic. I loved Mystic and its Main Street. It was a beautiful little town with cute pubs, restaurants, ice cream shops, and all kinds of eclectic boutiques and galleries. We walked past Mystic Pizza and crossed over the drawbridge to the other side of the river. On this side of the river, a gorgeous seafood restaurant stood right on the edge of the water.

When my ex boyfriend and I tired of Rhode Island, we visited Mystic. Even though I gazed longingly at this restaurant on the shore every time we passed it, he never took me there.

"Want to eat here?" he asked as we walked by.

My eyes widened. For the longest time I fantasized about eating *there*.

We sat outside at a high top table in a lush rose garden full of colorful blooms, different shades of red, yellow, and orange. It was a warm sunny day. Sitting so close together, our legs touched and every once in a while, he put his arm around me. Then he started again with the phone calls. After about 15 minutes, he finally put the it down.

"Why don't you take your sunglasses off?" I said sweetly. I wanted to see his eyes.

"I can't."

"Why?"

"I just can't."

"But you have such nice eyes, I just want to look at them. Why can't you?"

"Because my eyes are very...*sensitive*."

The food came and he ate about three bites of his meal. I did not eat much either, but only because every dish on the menu was made of some type of fish and I was a vegetarian.

Neither of us spoke much during lunch. He was fairly silent and I sat there thinking about heroine. *Heroine.* It was a strange name. Why had it been named *heroine* when it is more a destroyer of lives than a savior?

I was annoyed to share a definition with this drug. My name, "Hayley," came from the Norse word "haylo," which meant "hero." My name literally meant "heroine."

Later that night, I made him promise that if he was going to be with me, he would not do it again. It was not until the following morning that I realized that along with everything else he said and promised me, he was lying.

In the days of ancient mariners, the bows of great wooden ships were adorned with beautiful figureheads and often these figureheads were carved in the likeness of mermaids. These wooden merwomen were regarded as guardians of the crew, and treated with due respect. Like real mermaids, these figureheads protected sailors from harm and danger while out at sea.

He was a sailor, a fisherman, and here I was, some modern day mermaid, a heroine; just another woman who thought she would be the one for whom the bad boy would change. I wanted to be a beautiful mermaid, the figurehead of the old sailing ship, the angelic presence stretched across the bow of an ancient sailing vessel, protecting the crew, the men on their journey, keeping them safe. However I failed to acknowledge the old superstition: it was a bad omen if the men set off on their journey only to realize then that their beautiful figurehead was damaged.

V

Butterfly

This is a farce: all these will be my new relatives for only a month-

He was living in New York City. It was the early nineties, cocaine was big. At the time, he was too much into *the scene*. *She* wanted to marry him and have children, but he was not ready to marry her, so eventually, she married someone else.

Years later she contacted him one night, unhappy.

"It's *me*," she whispered into the phone.

"Honey, why you callin' me so late? Is everything alright?" he asked as she began to cry over the line.

"It's just that... I wish I'd married you."

"Come to Block Island, sweetie," she immediately obliged his invitation.

That weekend, they only left his bedroom during the afternoon hours to relax on the beach and soak in the the midday sun. She told her husband she was in Nantucket for the weekend with her girlfriends. Together again, it was as if no time passed and when the weekend concluded, she went home to her husband as if nothing ever happened. After that they never spoke again.

Though I never before viewed cheating without some level of disdain, I found this story to be oddly romantic. Though lust was his most prominent personality trait, it was lust of some strangely genuine variety. The story made me ache for the type of love affair movies are made of. After years of being bombarded with these types of stories in music, movies, and reality, how could I not want the same thing? Isn't that what everyone dreamed of ? The kind of love that inspires poetry?

He was the perfect character for my love story. He had an interesting life, a house on Block Island, his own business, and a posh apartment above the bar he worked at in Connecticut. Though he had slept with many young women, I hoped that maybe I would be the one he fell in love with.

He wanted to have sex with me. Over Instant Message, he begged me to sleep with him before we had even met in person, but when we did finally go out, he was on his best behavior.

We talked of marriage, he said he wanted a woman that he could spoil like a princess, someone who would stay at home and take care of his future children. I wanted this too, *well sort of.* I never wanted children, but sometimes things change, especially when you fall in love, *well that's what people told me.* And I did not want to give up my career. I worked from home, so maybe I could still do it while taking care of the children.

"You could work from Block or Connecticut," he said. "And maybe we could even open a little shop for you on the Island where you could sell your artwork."

Was he reading my mind?

"It would be the perfect arrangement," he continued.

I never expected to find such comfort in the idea of sharing my life so closely with someone else's, but now I did. And I always dreamed of having my own store. I did not doubt that he could make this happen. Whenever we went anywhere, he made sure I had whatever I needed. He made me feel taken care of and I had not felt like that in a while.

It was not just sex he craved, but romance. He liked to buy women flowers and to bring them to the beautiful places he enjoyed. He loved romantic dinners, bubble baths, walks on the beaches, and vacations. Oh. And he wanted to fuck. That was it. He did not just want cold hard sex, though. He wanted his sex laced with all the delicate and beautiful things that relationships were made of, but he did not want a relationship. He wanted a false romance. It did not make sense to me. It seemed he went through the all the motions, but was incapable of feeling.

We returned to his apartment after lunch and he asked me to stay even though he had to work. He invited me to hang out for a while and to have a few drinks at the bar while he bartended. Then he suggested I stay over.

"You expect me to just wait around all night for you to get out of work? I have a life, you know."

"No. Come downstairs and have a few drinks."

"Are you kidding? I'm not your groupie."

"It's not like that. It would just make me really happy if you stayed," he said putting his arms around me.

"You know that if I stay *nothing* is going to happen."

"Yeah, sure. That's fine," he gave me a gentle kiss.

"What am I suppose to do while you work?"

"I said, *come to the bar*."

He asked me to pick up a few things from the grocery before I went to the bar. I dutifully went to Stop and Shop to pick up his items. I played the role of girlfriend well and got exactly what was on the list: garbage bags, Drano, and toothpaste. I also got him a bag of peanut butter M&M's because I was trying to be sweet. After returning to his apartment and putting his stuff in the cupboards, I laid down on the couch to take a nap. He burst into the room with a cigarette hanging out of his mouth.

"Aren't you suppose to be working?" I asked.

"I'm on a break. I came up before but you weren't here. Why aren't you downstairs at the bar?"

"It's only 8 o'clock. I didn't want to bother you."

"*Just come,*" he said taking my hand in his and leading me down the stairs and into the pub.

As soon as we got down there, he introduced me to the regular patrons as his *girl* and his *girlfriend.* It felt amazing to be called someone's girlfriend again and even better, to be called it by him.

It seemed like my dreams were finally coming true. For the last year, as I traversed the beaches looking for sea glass, I dreamed of one day finding a partner that I could share my life with. I dreamed of moving with them closer to the shore. I could not believe how things had turned around for me. Now I was dating a guy who had a home on Block Island, a guy who kept talking to me about marriage! So far, everything was perfect.

He was handsome and a good kisser. I wanted to sleep with him. By the merit of his kissing, I was sure he was good at other things. He thought my braids were hot and that made me feel sexy. I fantasized about the life we would have together on Block Island, how he would take care of me, and how I would love him back. I pictured myself in our cute colonial on Block. Walking through the sunshine with a baby in my arms, I waded through long blades of beach grass to greet him as he came home from work.

Though he painted a good picture of the future, none of it had happened yet. I could not bring myself to hook up with him... *not casually.* Not until I knew he would not leave. I wanted him to fall in love with me the way I was starting to fall in love with him. Still, I could not throw myself into a physical relationship with him or anyone regardless of my feelings. I craved monogamy and needed fidelity. Sex was a part of every one of my meaningless relationships and I just did not want that anymore. I wanted it to mean something again.

Knowing what I knew of him, I could not help question his sincerity. I could not take that chance with him and risk being thrown out like garbage; tossed into the sea like trash, left to meander down the shore, and float aimlessly until I got stuck on a jagged rock for all eternity or until I disintegrated and wasted away.

When the bar closed, I hung out while he cleaned. He still had to count the cash drawer, but decided he would do it later. We left the bar and went up to his apartment and watched movies. After his friend left, we cuddled and made out. He told me again about what he wanted in a wife: a woman who would stay home and take care of the children in their house on Block Island. *Ok already, I get it; it will be perfect!*

Everything was going awesome until I misspoke and unknowingly sparked an argument over drugs. He told me a story about a cop who had been harassing him while he was high.

"Well that is the cop's job," I began, "I mean, if you're gonna get high, you should not go out in public. Especially not around cops --- if you don't want to get in trouble."

"I can't believe you are taking the cop's side!" He shouted at me, his Rhode Island accent sharper than ever.

"What? No I'm not. I was just saying that if anything, you should be happy that he didn't arrest you."

I could not believe how quickly he got so mad. It was shocking that what I said so innocently had set him off to this degree.

"I need someone who's gonna be on *my team,* not someone who love *pigs,*" he stormed back down to the bar to finish counting the money.

He left in a fury and I sat on his futon crying.

Forty-five minutes passed. The sunlight begin to peer through the blinds. I climbed down the rickety wooden stairs to the pub. It was frigid out and I was just wearing a tank top and shorts, the only outfit I had with me --- the one I wore to lunch.

I peered in through the bar's picture window. He stood behind the bar counting the money. I knocked on the glass. He looked up and gave me an evil glare. He dropped his head and then walked over to the door. I heard him unlock the deadbolt. The door swung open.

"You know that now I am going to have to do that all over again. It is going to be another hour before I'm done because you interrupted me."

His Yankee accent was now hard edged and nasty.

"I'm... I'm sorry," I stammered, "I, I just didn't want you to be mad at me."

He groaned and shut the door in my face. I ran back upstairs to the apartment and began to cry. Should I leave? *Probably.* Instead I washed all the dishes in his entire sink still desperately seeking his love and approval.

Eventually he came upstairs. He walked in the door and noticed the bag of peanut M&M's sitting on the counter.

"You got these for me?"

He melted a little.

"Yeah."

He went into the bedroom and went to sleep.

"I guess I will just go home now..."

"No come here," he said, as I dutifully crawled into his bed wearing my tank top and shorts. He put his arm around me and apologized.

"I did the dishes," I responded.

"You did?"

"Yeah."

"That's so sweet, *thank-you.*"

We kissed.

"I'm sorry I got mad at you," he spoke calmly now, "I just really need someone who is going to be on my team."

I made excuses for him in my head. I blamed myself. *I was not supportive,* he was correct, but still, *he should not have acted like that.* He should not have yelled at me. We cuddled until we fell asleep in each others arms.

The following morning, he began to make demands on me. I needed to "sexually pleasure him," he said.

"Are you joking? Umm, no."

"Then you need to leave," he growled grabbing my hand and shoving it down his boxers.

"Stop!" I shouted, grabbing my hand back and away from his dick.

"What's your problem? Are you afraid of the penis?" He taunted me.

"Maybe you should date a priest!" He stood up abruptly and stormed into the bathroom. "Just leave!" His accent was strong again, the meaner he was, the harsher it got.

"Leave?"

Was this not the same man who less than 24 hours before sat next to me on the outdoor patio eating a beautiful lunch on the Mystic River? Was this not the same man whose hand and mine intertwined meeting and then parting only to meet again as we picked at out appetizers?

I thought about it. The whole scenario was odd, but I could not figure out why. He had worn sunglasses the entire afternoon even though I asked him to remove them. I also thought it was odd that he asked me to drive.

Initially, he asked me to stop by because his friend had been killed in an accident days earlier. I had been nothing but understanding about his friend's death, even though it was my birthday. I thought maybe he would at the very least, acknowledge it, but he did not. To ease my disappointment, I told myself that the afternoon we dined in Mystic was my official birthday lunch. I did not press the issue, that he did not sing let alone say "Happy birthday" to me. I reminded myself that he seemed to be grieving.

"I can't look at you! You make me sick," he shouted from the bathroom.

Now I was perplexed. The night before, he said that he liked me because I was "a *good girl,* not a *whore* like all the other ones," and now he was getting mad at me for not putting out.

The night before, it all meshed so well. He said that he liked me, but had no indication how I felt about him. I played it off slyly, and said that I was not sure how I felt about him. This, of course, was a lie and he believed me. In fact, *every time* I lied to him, he believed me. No matter how ridiculous, he received each one of my fallacies with a straight face. He was completely unable to detect any of my lies which led me to believe that he was obviously lying, too.

When he calmed down, he invited me to his bar later that night. He suggested I bring a friend and even said that he would leave his apartment unlocked for me if we wanted to wait there for him instead of going to the bar.

That night, I drove to Stonington to console my cousin who had coincidentally just been dumped. She was house sitting at a beach house. It was nighttime.

We sat outside on the deck. She sobbed as I stared off into the Sound. I listened quietly and watched as the reflection of stars occasionally flickered on the water's surface. She told me his story: an Iraq Vet, injured in the war, and addicted to painkillers.

Together, we smoked a pack of Lucky Strikes and drank robust red wine while we whined about our man problems. Then her man problem showed up. He seemed nice enough and was even a bit concerned about me. He did not think it was a good idea for me to go back to the bar.

"Sounds like he just wants sex and is trying to pressure you, *this is coming from a guy's perspective.*"

"I hate that, guys are so...ugh."

"Yeah, well. It sucks 'cuz sometimes women are like that too," he said glancing towards my cousin.

I felt like it was time to go. I drove back down I-95 towards my house. I would inevitably pass close by his exit on the way home. The whole drive back I debated. Should I or shouldn't I? And then when I saw the sign for his exit, without thinking I pulled off at it and drove towards his street.

When I arrived at the bar, though he mixed me drinks and smiled, he did not seem happy to see me. I sat next to a married blond woman. We were chatting and having a good time until she wrote her number down on a piece of paper and handed it to him right in front of me. She was a good friend of his neighbor's and that night she happened to be sleeping over his neighbor's house.

When the bar finally closed, she and I were the last people to leave. I waited her out. After dwindling well past closing, she finally left.

As soon as she shut the door behind her, he screamed at me, "Why are you here?"

"You invited me!"

He did not respond and just looked at me angrily.

"You even promised to leave the door to your apartment open for me, *remember*?"

"Yes," he shook his head.

"Well, did you leave it unlocked? I'm too drunk to drive home *now.*"

He looked up from what he was doing behind the bar and evilly glared at me. When he went into the back room, I bolted. Though I had left my sunglasses at his place, I decided that it was time to forfeit them as well as anything else I had given him.

I drove home that night with more alcohol in me than I would typically drive with. He never called, not even to see if I got home safely. I imagined that

143

he so badly wanted me to leave because he planned on hooking up with the blond after he closed the bar that night. *Nah.* Why would he want to mess around with some middle-aged married woman who had a dozen kids?

The next day, he instant messaged me and hounded me again about blow jobs. I tried to change the subject, but he kept asking me if I could deep throat.

"You're sick," I responded.

"Can you?"

"That's privileged information."

"I bet you can..."

"Just tell me one thing. Why didn't you want me to stay the other night?"

He ignored my question and redirected the conversation again to the subject of fellatio technique. And then it dawned on me, "You hooked up with that blond chick didn't you?"

"She gave me a blow job," he said, "but she couldn't take it all in like you probably can. *You should show me sometime.*"

"Really?"

"Yes. Come over now."

"No asshole. You *really* hooked up with her?"

"I was kidding..."

"Right..."

Regardless of what he said now, it was too late. I knew the truth. I knew he did. He even admitted it, *initially.*

He said he snorted it. Why did the fact that he did not use a needle make it better in my mind? *Heroine.* Did I secretly harbor a death wish? Though I refused to entertain his physical demands, I had wanted to. After our lunch in Mystic we went back to his apartment and cuddled on the couch. He kissed me slowly. His pace soon accelerated. He took his hand and grabbed a fist full of my long mermaid braids and gently pulled back my head to kiss my throat.

He said he had gotten tested and that everything was negative. I did not believe him. Maybe everything was negative, but I doubt he had gotten tested. He said he had not had sex in over a year, but less than a week after we stopped talking, he changed his Facebook profile picture to a shot of himself with a beautiful brunette, whose breasts were popping out of her shirt, draped over one of his arms and an adorable blond draped on the other. Both looked about 18, *19 at the oldest.*

I was torn. I wanted to have a love affair, but the lack of security always kept me from doing so. I needed the assurance that they would not kick me out of their place the morning after for refusing to *pleasure* them. I wanted them to value me as a person, not as a reliable lay for the nights that they could not find someone else to fuck. I could not risk giving my soul to a man like him; a man who might never call me again, a man who had already broken every promise he had ever made. Most of all, I did not want to be somebody's nobody.

I was bummed for the next week, well crushed really. I retired our future life on Block Island to the category of permanent daydreams; another little piece of my heart that had not exactly been taken, but willfully given away, all because I hoped that this time things might be different.

One afternoon, I rambled on to my aunt, "It's so weird --- that I have never been to Block Island, never even gave visiting Block any serious thought until a few months ago when I was invited and then uninvited to that beach party and then a second time when I met Mr. "let me take you on a private plane to show you my summer home on Block." Now, I have not only almost been to Block Island, but I have almost been to Block Island more than once, and I still have not ended up getting there at all. To be honest, this was much worse than where I began: having never had the opportunity nor thought to actually go to Block Island in the first place."

"Hmmm. Are you listening to what you're saying?" she asked. "*Block* Island? Maybe it's called *Block* Island for a reason. Maybe you're *not* suppose to go there."

I thought about what she said. I mumbled to myself a bit. There was no point in disputing her carefully crafted comment.

"It just irritates me," I began, "that people like him get everything they want in life."

"He doesn't *get* everything he wants, he takes it!"

Later that day I got a call from my cousin. She was crying. The veteran had broken up with her again. She was in love with him, she said, in love with a veteran who was addicted to pain meds because of a debilitating war injury. He was miserable and depressed and no matter what she did, he could not function in his relationship with her. He could not handle conflict of any kind and would shut down or worse, shut her out at the smallest complaint.

I thought for a moment. I too was mourning the loss of a relationship. In that short period, I had fallen extremely hard for *him* or the him he portrayed himself to be.

"Well maybe he can't love you because he doesn't love himself," I said to her regarding her veteran.

And then it hit me. With one short sentence, I had answered both her problem and mine. It did not matter that he would never like me, let alone love me. He could never love anyone. Why was I mourning what could have been, but never was? What was I mourning? A fake romance? A dream?

After this final crushing defeat, I began to reevaluate things. It was weird. There was so much about his lifestyle I wanted. I missed bartending. I wanted to live on the beach. I wanted my own place. I had been dreaming of moving closer to the shoreline before and after he ever existed in my life. I finally started to realize that even before he showed up, I had been relying on my connections with men and the possibility of a future with them to get there. I did not need a man to help find my way to the ocean. I never had. I could find a way to get down there on my own. It was around this time I answered an ad on Craigslist for a bartending job and I got the surprise of my life.

I remember when I was in elementary school, one of my friends told me that when she was on vacation at Disney World, if someone asked where she was from and she told them she was from Connecticut, they immediately assumed she was rich. I was perplexed. She had an in-ground pool but certainly did not live in a gated community. Our families were from working class Waterbury neighborhoods.

I discovered when I went to an out of state college that what she said was true, that when you tell people you are from Connecticut they assume you live in a neighborhood on par with one of the most affluent ones in Greenwich. Years ago, I had never been to Greenwich and wondered what this place was like. The richest

town in the entire country would surely be something worth checking out. I

imagined that I would be pegged an outsider from the second my 2001 Kia

Sportage crossed over and into the city limits.

For a while now, I had been working for a holistic beauty company and

had to go to various health food retailers. Because of this job, I drove down

towards the Gold Coast for work at least once a month. My first experience there

was good and not at all like the caricature of the rich snobbish community of

people that outsiders portrayed and expected it to be.

After coming across an ad on Craigslist for a bartender, I quickly sent out

my resume and a photo and was hired immediately. The man I spoke to asked if I

would be able to come down the next day. Not only would I be bartending in

Greenwich, but on a yacht!

I would be lying if I told you I was excited. No, I reacted as I usually do

when something really great and exciting happens in my life: I was terrified! I had

never answered an ad on Craigslist before and feared it was not legit. A yacht?

Really? As usual, I pictured worst-cases-scenarios in my head; the yacht taking off

with me and other unsuspecting young "bartenders" on it, carrying us out to sea

where we awaited some sort of mass-auction, our introduction into sexual slavery.

I do not deny that I am *a little* crazy. I lived on the Mexican border for a

year and never ventured south for the same reason. It's funny how someone who

has lived to tell the tale of so many risky and dangerous events can be so scared and cautious. I would wager that it is because *I lived to tell the tale of so many risky and dangerous events.*

I drove to the address the next morning and did not see any yachts. It took me a while to find the place: a shipyard. Once I arrived, I found that I was locked out, of course. The entire marina was gated.

Someone let me in and I began to drive around the lot. The place was huge with many elegant yachts resting high in the air on stilts. I could not help but picture myself driving into them by accident. Just one quick jolt of the wheel and there would be irreparable damage. Perhaps this is why so many things in Greenwich were gated. It was the whole hot stove theory and I could not help thinking about the very thing I should never do.

I finally found the ship. I could not miss it. It looked more like a cruise ship than a yacht. That day I watched as they loaded up the ship with art. Men pushed small sculptures of solid marble up the ramp while others carried large canvases concealed by a protective cardboard barriers.

It was not just a yacht, it was one of the largest privately owned yachts in the world; a yacht built for the sole purpose of hosting art galleries. It stopped at different ports as it traveled down the East Coast. Three floors were filled with galleries from across the country and the world. It was no small show. It included works from the likes of Warhol and even Picasso. It did not take many days before I started to wish I was on the other side of the bar.

The art was not the only attraction at the show, in fact, I think I had more fun looking at the different jewelry on the women as they walked by. Some of

them were draped in gold, delicate necklaces that covered their entire chests. And

the size of their emeralds were cartoonish, not that I would not have wanted one of

these huge emerald cut matchbooks. There were necklaces with bloodstones the

size of baseballs. I had always had a thing for jewelery.

One day I decided to wear a huge cocktail ring to work. It was as big as

the emeralds I had seen, but it was yellow. *I hope this doesn't make me look cheap,*

I thought to myself, completely disregarding the bright orange lipstick I had also

applied earlier that morning.

After opening the bar that afternoon, it did not take very long, for people

to notice it. I crouched down to pull a bottle of chardonnay out of the fridge. As I

began to twist the corkscrew, I heard,

"That's a beautiful ring," from the patron above me.

I did not know what to say.

"Thanks," this was almost comical, well, *to me it was.*

The woman did not take her eye off it as I handed her the glass of wine.

She and her friend continued to fawn over it as I outstretched my hand for them to

see. If it was a real stone it would have easily exceeded 10 carats. And its yellow

color was more on par with a canary diamond than something more affordable like

citrine. Then they noticed my earrings: more costume jewelry that I purchased at

Macy's. They were beautiful green emeralds with strands of smaller emeralds and peridots cascading off of them.

"Someone must really like you!" they said.

I laughed at that thought. I had been single for a while and my last boyfriend, never bought me a single piece of jewelry. In fact, I had considered dumping him the summer we began dating after he cited that engagement rings were a "stupid waste of money." I balked at his comment.

"What?" I said, irritated.

We were driving to Rhode Island to stay over for Fourth of July weekend. It was a Friday afternoon and the traffic was already completely backed up making it the worst possible time for him to bring this into the conversation: today this hour and a half car ride that would surely take four.

"What do you mean engagement rings are a *waste of money*."

"Why should I have to buy a stupid ring to show someone them that I love them?"

"Because it's tradition!"

I did not even buy what I was saying; nothing about me had ever been traditional and here I was arguing for tradition. What can I say, *I wanted a diamond.*

"That's ridiculous. I expect the guy I am going to marry to buy me a huge emerald cut diamond with a yellow gold band, a thick yellow gold band, and perhaps some type of romantic engraving on the inside, but I will leave the exact inscription up to him."

He ignored me. At this point, I did not believe what I was saying either. I gave him the description of a beautiful ring, the most beautiful ring I could think of; something a princess would wear --- no a queen. What woman did not want to feel like royalty, at least to one person in the world? So I did it. I named off the specifications of an engagement ring that would cost way more than he could ever afford, in the upwards of ten thousand dollars depending on the clarity and you know what? I did it on purpose.

I did not want to marry him. I knew it then and that was my little way of slipping in a stipulation that would make me an impossible fish for him to ever catch. I would be lying again if I said what he said did not make me sad. It did. It made me feel worthless. At least lie to me, at least try, pretend, pretend that you will do everything in your power to make me feel like the most special woman you have ever met. Is it that difficult?

He was the one who asked me out. I would never hold it against a man if he could not afford to buy me something, especially if his feelings were genuine. Unfortunately (or maybe fortunately) he had neither *genuine feelings for me nor money to buy me anything.*

He was so romantic. To be honest, I could care less about an engagement ring. I did not need a guy to buy me diamonds. In fact, I would rather buy them for myself any day before I would accept them from a man who was just using me. At this point, I was resigned to the idea that maybe I would be alone *forever.*

"Do you have a boyfriend?" she pried.

"No," I laughed. *Just rub it in, lady! Oh, and I am childless as well, don't remember the last time I had sex, and I had an abnormal pap-smear a few months ago, but don't worry, if I'm lucky that one might just be a lab-tech error.*

"They were gifts from my aunt," I said mustering a smile.

The night continued on as did the never-ending stream of compliments and looks of awe directed at my jewelry. If I had worn the same jewelry in Waterbury, people would have known it was fake, but in Greenwich, people did not suspect a thing. It was a case of psychological transference at its best.

I felt slightly embarrassed (I was always a little shy). However, I was not so foolish that I did not appreciate being "Queen for a Day." I knew that by the time I got back to Waterbury, after my hour and a half-long commute, my coach would turn back into a pumpkin once again.

That night after work, I walked into the house, threw my wad of tips onto the bathroom counter and looked in the mirror. Yup. I was still single, still alone, and leaning into my reflection in the bathroom mirror covered in fake jewels: there were no glass slippers, no prince, not even a friendly mouse. Nope. Just some pathetic modern day Macy's-Three-Day-Sale version of Miss Havisham.

I hated being alone. *Hated it.* Soon one of the guys on the ship, a crew member, took a liking to me. One morning, as I walked to the top deck and swung my purse behind the my bar I heard him say.

"You look beautiful today, Hayley."

I looked up and smiled. A few nights later, us bartenders went out one night with the crew to a few bars in downtown Stamford. His eyes were squinty, which made me a little suspicious, but his words seemed genuine. I suspected he was a player, part of me did; he just had the look in his eye --- the gleam, the narrowness of them.

One of the bartenders I worked with warned me that a few days before he had said she was the hottest girl on the ship, but I did not care. He did not call me hot. He used a more refined adjective for me. He said I was *beautiful*.

That night, while the group of us were at the bar, he sat next to me and attempted to put his arm around me at every opportunity.

"You know I meant it the other day, when I said you looked beautiful."

I wondered why he was expressing this to me as I never questioned his sincerity nor was I interested enough to even think about questioning it in the first place.

"It wasn't just some line. *I meant it,*" he continued, "I thought you looked beautiful."

"Thanks," I said wondering how long he was gonna drag this out.

"I really meant it... I mean, I just don't look at women the same...ever since I had my twin *daughters*."

It was *that* phrase in particular that got me. After that night, we spent more time together on the ship. When it was slow at the bar, I would text him and ask him to come visit me. When he had a minute, he would come by to chat until one of his supervisors showed up, *then he would have to try to look busy.*

Soon the ship would be sailing to its next port. As the days dwindled, my affection for him grew inversely. I pictured the great potential of this love affair and the longing that would surely ensue if I fell in love with a seaman.

In *Madame Butterfly,* the main character, Butterfly, falls hard for her husband to be, US Navy Lieutenant Pinkerton. Little does she know that this American views her as a *one in every port* and believes that "life is not worth living if he can't win the best and fairest of each country, and the heart of each maid." However, this attitude does not prevent Pinkerton from pursuing and proposing marriage to Butterfly.

As we became better friends, he told me more about his daughters. Then one of the bartenders told me that she overheard him talking to another crew member about his twin's mother: that he had wanted to marry her and still would if she would have him. This news did not bode well for whatever intentions he had for me, but then again, this was the same bartender who claimed he had called her hot. I shook off my concern, she was probably jealous. Besides, he was here and his ex-girlfriend was in Florida. He would not be seeing her for several more months.

In *Madame Butterfly,* the American Consul talks to Pinkerton about his pending matrimony with Butterfly. During this conversation, Pinkerton's true intentions are revealed: they are as fleeting as is his deployment to Japan. Though he planned to show her affection, he had no plans of taking his marriage to her seriously. It was not that he did not want her, he did. He did not look at Butterfly as a wife, but as a conquest. He knew that her feelings for him were genuine and that he would cause her much pain when he left Japan for The States. He also knew that after his departure, they might never speak again.

She did not question his intentions and had no inkling that he had no intentions of carrying out his duties as husband. She did not know what pain would surely ensue for her. He laughs as he brags to the American Consul, "Butterfly," he says is an appropriate name for her because like a butterfly she is beautiful yet frail, and in "my quest for her, her frail wings should be broken. To think that pretty plaything is my wife! My wife!"

The other bartender from the ship and I decided to go to NYC and spend the night partying into the early morning hours. The ship's crew members wanted to come along and agreed to meet up with us on the train. We were surprised when we boarded the train and were greeted only by *him* and his cabin mate, who had a crush on my companion. From the moment we were seated, it was evident by his friend's eyes that he was blazed.

"I'm glad *you* choose not to smoke," I whispered into my date's ear.

He put his arm around me as the train took off from Greenwich Station and continued towards Grand Central Terminal. We exited the train and got onto a subway. As we rode the car to the West Village, he ran his fingers through my hair.

"Your hair is so dark and shiny like lacquer," he commented.

"I love it when a guy does that," I said.

"Does what?" he asked.

"Runs his fingers through my hair."

"Really?"

"Yes."

"Some women don't like it."

"Really?" I said perplexed.

"Yup. My baby's mama hates it. *She isn't very affectionate.*"

I cringed every time he used the phrase "baby's mama." It was so white trash. He seemed like a good guy, but very blue collar. Never been to college. Did not even finish middle school. It did not matter to me. At this point, I began to think that as long as a man treated me well little else mattered.

For dinner, the four of us went to a Mexican restaurant where the guys took shots of Patron and we sipped generously portioned pina coladas. The more he drank, the more he talked about his family. The twins lived somewhere in Florida with his *baby's mama* who was pregnant again with another man's child. He really loved them and was sad that they could not "stay a family."

He had spent the entire year on the ship traveling up and down the East Coast. His true home was no longer in Florida or anywhere on land, but on the ship in a room with no windows. Regardless of his residence, it seemed he was trying to strike up something with me here in Connecticut.

Pinkerton laughed again as he and the Consul continued drinking. The only thing he regards as traditional about his upcoming nuptials is the idea that it is customary for an American Naval Lieutenant to woo an Asian woman, marry her, and then dump her when he returned home to America. Conveniently for him, even the Japanese marriage contract made carrying out this plan convenient and provided him the opportunity to cancel the marriage monthly.

The talk of his *baby's mama* was starting to worry me, but the fact that he had been so attentive and sweet to me gave me confidence. I already knew I would never be number one in his life because he had children, but I was willing to accept second place in return for his love. Wasn't love all about sacrifice? And even though my family said it was a bad idea, I was seriously considering carrying out my longtime plan of moving to the shore and buying myself a condo *in Florida.*

Pinkerton discusses his future plans for Butterfly with the American Consul shortly before what Butterfly views as a very real wedding commences. The Consul warns Pinkerton that her feelings for him may be very real and that his absence may cause her much damage. He ignores the warning, and sticks to his plans to divorce Butterfly when he gets back to the United States. As Butterfly's family begins to arrive at the ceremony, Pinkerton raises his glass to the Consul and makes a toast, a toast to the day he finds a *real American wife.*

It was a weeknight, which meant the trains did not run late. The last train was coming soon, not long after we had arrived in the city --- soon, *as in two hours after we got there soon.* Rather than leave then, the boys wanted to take a taxi back to Connecticut a little later. They told us that a taxi back would cost $25 a person. My friend and I exchanged perturbed glances.

"We're good," I said, "but if you want to, you can go back without us."

We already bought our return ticket for the train and had made plans to ride out the night and take the first train back early the next morning. Because they had to work the next morning, they were reluctant to stay out all night with us, but even more reluctant to spend $50 each for a cab ride home.

We spent the next several hours crisscrossing the city by foot and taxi. We went to lounges, nightclubs, and hookah bars. By 3 AM, cockroaches and mice ran in circles in front of us as we traversed the sidewalk. I cringed at the sight of the roaches.

At one point, he and I got separated from the other two. Unsure of where to go, we continued walking down a cobblestone street in the Village. Still, neither of us knew where we were. We walked hand in hand until suddenly, a nicely dressed black man appeared out of nowhere and flanked the other side of him like the devil on his shoulder.

"Free samples, *cocaine and marijuana*," he said.

"What the fuck?" I muttered turning my head to look.

We had discussed many things in our short friendship and cocaine was one of them. He knew how much I liked it, *no scratch that,* loved it. In fact, I liked it so much that I promised myself for the rest of my life I would stay away from it.

"Keep walking," I said, but then my companion unexpectedly let go of my hand. He stopped in the middle of the sidewalk and put out his fist to the stranger, who poured a small line of white powder onto his hand. I continued walking but looked back and watched as the cocaine disappeared up his nose.

"Are you crazy?" I asked him when he finally caught up with me.

"What?"

"That guy could've been an undercover. You could've got us both arrested! This is New York City. There are cameras everywhere!"

It was true that there were cameras everywhere. We had even seen what looked like undercover Homeland Security earlier in the night in Time's Square. We turned the corner and unexpectedly ran back into our friends. They were cheerful and could not understand why I was so pissed off. Not only had my date snorted a line of coke while we were standing in the middle of a public boulevard, but he also bought two grams from the guy.

We walked until we found a small coffee shop. Its brightly glowing fluorescent lights pierced my eyes as we sat there groggily eating our bagels. My former companion disappeared into the cafe's bathroom every ten minutes while the rest of us sat quietly awaiting 5:30 AM.

On the walk to Grand Central Terminal, he kept trying to hold my hand and I kept trying to avoid his.

"I told you, I don't date people who do drugs," *not after what happened the last time.*

"But Hayley, it's not *that* big of a deal."

"Whatever. You have kids. That's $80 you could've spent on them," I stopped in front of a large trash can. "If you want to date me you can throw it out now."

He stared at the can in silence.

"All I have to say is that someone with kids should be a little more discreet- because believe me, they will find out *eventually.*"

We got onto the train. I was done lecturing him, but now I was even more pissed off that he did not throw the coke out. I was sleepy, too; we all were, it being so very early in the morning. On the train, he kept trying to rest his head on my shoulder to nap.

"Get off of me," I said shoving him away.

He pulled out a pack of gum, I glared at it. My mouth was *so* dry.

"Can I have a piece?"

"Sure," he said and put the stick between his teeth and waited. "You have to come get it," he cooed.

Despite my anger, I could not help but find this move really sexy, but I was too frustrated to let him know it. I scrunched up my nose and glared at him.

"Will you just hand it to me?" I asked with an attitude.

Later that day, he texted me. He claimed that he had thought about what I said and that if it "was going to work out between us" he would get rid of it. He said that if I wanted him to flush it, he would. Then he texted me a picture of tiny baggie half full of blow floating in a toilet. "I did this for us," he had written at the bottom of the text. *For us?* Was this suppose to be some shade of romantic? It was not. However, the thought that there was or was not going to be an *us* suddenly made it easy to overlook his cocaine digression, *just that once.*

Neither he nor the yacht would be in Greenwich for long. It would soon be *en route* down the East Coast to South Carolina. The ship would continue setting up art galleries in different ports until it reached its final destination, Florida. It mainly stopped at wealthy port-side communities and before Greenwich, it had been docked in Newport, Rhode Island. The other bartenders and I made arrangements with the captain to meet the ship at their next port where they were holding a huge festival. Unlike in Greenwich, this time we would be raking the money in because down there they knew how to party.

We even talked to the captain about staying down south for the next few months to work all their ports in Florida. I wanted to move to Florida for a while and maybe this was my chance. Now I knew people that lived down there, *I had made friends with the entire crew,* and maybe I would even have a boyfriend once

I got there.

Things were looking up. Life was beginning to feel exciting again. I was over the last guy and feeling independent. My family was a little concerned about my motivations for leaving, though I reminded them that I had been planning to move closer to the shore for more than a year now.

It became obvious to the American Consul and to Butterfly's friends and family that she looked at the marriage as a marriage and not the temporary Japanese arrangement that Pinkerton viewed it as. Butterfly was very much in love with Pinkerton. She converted to his religion in order to marry him and by doing so, unknowingly alienated her entire kin. She took with her only a few of her most treasured possessions including the long sheath that her father used to commit suicide.

The marriage ceremony commences and she is introduced by her bridesmaids, her slightly jealous cousins. When her family learns that she converted to his *American* religion in order to marry him, her uncle interrupts the celebration and causes a huge scene. Pinkerton throws the family out and is left to console his sobbing new wife.

With everyone gone, the bride and groom are finally alone. Butterfly confesses that she was not initially interested in marrying him, but then she fell in love. In a prayer, she begs that at the very least he love her 'just a little." Gently, he refers to her as "his butterfly." She recoils at the thought.

"They say in your country, if a butterfly is caught by a man, he'll pierce its heart with a needle and leave it to perish!"

He tells her that she has nothing to worry about.

Eventually he has to leave on the ship, but promises Butterfly he will be back when "the robins nest."

The night before the ship departed, I visited him to say goodbye. He wanted to kiss me, to give him "a *goodbye* kiss," he said. I refused, but would soon regret it.

"I'll see you in South Carolina," I said as I got into my truck and drove away.

Everyday thereafter, he called to tell me that he missed me. "He was thinking about me," he would say. Each evening, he would text me a picture of the sunset from whichever harbor they were docked at for the night. "I wish you were here watching this with me," he would write underneath the photos of the sunset. The colors of the setting sun vibrated behind the silhouettes of boats, masts, and docks. From the glow of my smart phone, I stared at the vibrant oranges and reds and began to wonder if I was the only woman he had been texting these to.

While I waited for the call to go down to South Carolina, I daydreamed about the life we would have together. We even talked about weddings. Both of us dreamed of getting married on the beach and coincidentally, out of all the beaches in the world, we both shared the same favorite: Clearwater Beach in Florida.

I imagined what it would be like once I moved down there, once I moved in with him. I had visited many beaches in Florida, but did not have time to scour them for sea glass. I envisioned mountains of white sand glittering with turquoise, teals, and blue pieces of glass that shone through the sand like lost treasure as we strolled together through the magnificent sunset to look for them.

My grandmother had a hope chest. The way its dark stained wooden planks were bound together with strips of steal made it look more like a treasure chest than something that belonged to a grandmother. This chest, held together by rivets, was not the most refined and came from the Baltic region of Poland, where she came from too.

Like my grandmother, an entire generation of young unmarried women, as well as many generations before them, stored household items and linens in hope chests while they anticipated a future where they would one day be married. Until recently, on most days, I barely had hope, *let alone a chest full of it.* The concept itself died out along with the youth of my grandmother's era. What I did have was a big plastic tote container filled with linens, pottery, and other stuff for the kitchen I did not have.

When I was a small child, my grandmother always reminded me that when she died, she was going to leave me her Lenox dishes. At the time, I did not know what Lenox dishes were. She owned the entire classic Christmas set that Lenox sold for decades. Each piece of fine china was decorated by hand-painted holly berries and finished off with gold plated rims.

"Thanks a lot, mom," my aunt would say jealously half-joking, "*she* gets the dishes. She's only eight years old, what is *she* going to do with them?"

I was wondering the same thing, to be honest.

I spent my 21st birthday in my aunt's living room sitting with my grandmother, who lay in a hospital bed in the middle of the room slowly dying from cancer. A few weeks after her death, when I was clearing out her apartment, I found a big box full of Lenox dishes. I took home the set of Lenox Christmas dishes along with several boxes of ornately decorated Depression Glass. Some of the dishes were translucent reds, some were crystal with pink roses. It was difficult to believe that during The Great Depression, places like cinemas and grocery stores gave away these beautiful pieces of glassware for free.

Since then, I amassed a large collection of useless home goods in the same style my cousins, three tyrannical nerds, amassed territories every Christmas Eve, as they sat on the living room rug endlessly playing Risk. Certainly every boyfriend I have ever had had a mother who added to my stash. I could tell by their gifts that these women aimed at domesticating me. One large crystal trifle dish. A set of sushi making tools and a hand-sewn apron. A granite mortar and pestle. All beautiful gifts with no home or chest to put them in.

Over the next several years, I bought more home goods. Cozy over-sized ceramic bowls and coffee mugs. A hand blown glass pitcher from the Jamestown Settlement in Virginia. My favorite home good conquests of all were the hand-sewn table cloths I purchased in Greece and Malta. Each linen draped in detailed embroidery down to the last corner. Olives on one, blue roses with silver threading on another, and of course, one with a large Maltese cross tatted in the center.

When I bought these items, I did not realize that I would one day have a stack of table cloths, but no table to put them on. No home of my own or anyone to share one with. For years, these beautiful pieces of fabric sat unused in boxes in my closet next to my other treasures. Perhaps these items were the fuel that propelled my domestic daydreams.

And then we got the news. We would not be rehired to work in Florida or even South Carolina. He was as disappointed as I, but continued to call me anyways. He promised that in a few months he would try to buy a plane ticket so he could fly to New York to see me. I understood that most of his money went to his twins and because of that I would have to wait until he had extra cash to buy a plane ticket to see him. I did not mind waiting patiently if his feelings for me were true.

My girlfriend, the other bartender told me not to bother to wait around.

"I'd be shocked if he ever came back if not for more work on the ship." I glared at her. "Once he gets back to his home state and hooks back up with his *baby's mama,* I doubt you'll hear from him again."

I did not respond.

"Don't pout," she continued, "you never know, *he might come back.* In the meantime though, if I were you, I'd date that cute hedge fund manager we met at The Spotted Pig last weekend. Hasn't he been calling you ever since?"

I rolled my eyes.

"He seemed really nice," she added.

Unlike myself, she had no idea how deep *his* feelings ran for me. Besides, I did not know what a hedge fund was and to me, the very idea of dating a hedge fund manager did not sound too romantic. Now, I deeply regretted not letting him kiss me goodbye.

Things were as good as they could be, now that we were over a thousand miles apart. The fact that he was still interested even though neither of us knew when we would see each other next, made me feel better. I did not start to wonder about our status until his *baby's mama* started to come back into the conversation.

Every day he sent me texts saying how lucky he was to have a girl like me and how he wished I could have came down to South Carolina. He missed me and said that he could not wait until the day he got to see me again.

"Don't forget me," he said.

How could I? He was the most romantic guy I had ever met. The texts he sent and times he called to tell me he was thinking about me put him in a category that easily surpassed any of my exes.

More days passed. Now that the ship was docked in South Carolina, he was working full time and I did not hear from him much. For days I waited for him to call. He finally called me one night, from the top deck, drunk and talkin' dirty to me, but other than that, I did not hear much else from him.

I did notice that he had new female Facebook friends; were they the new bartenders who were working on the ship at this new port? Had I so easily been replaced? These fears made something that the last I guy I dated said echo in my mind. That morning when he kicked me out of his place for refusing to *pleasure* him, we got into a disagreement.

"I thought you said I was special. That there was something different about me."

"Everyone can be replaced," the phrase seemed to slither off his tongue.

It felt like he was pulling away from me and I did not like it. I was not sure if it was because he was busy working or worse. Either way, he had been too busy to call me much. I had been slowly opening my heart to him over the last few weeks and now I felt a bit... foolish.

One afternoon, he finally called me. When he called me, he said that he had been thinking about me.

This time I said it, "I was thinking about you were you thinking about me?"

"To be honest," he began, "I've been so busy lately that I haven't really thought much of you. I've just been worrying about the twins and everything. My baby's mama suspects I'm talking to someone new," he said with a slight southern drawl. "And said if I am, she's not going to send me anymore pictures of the children."

"That's horrible."

"Yeah, she's pretty manipulative. She keeps telling me how much she *needs* me in her life and how much she misses talking to me. *If you need someone to be there for you that's something you need to take up with your boyfriend,* I told her, before hanging up the phone."

Something about him had changed, but I was not sure what. After his admission I could not help but ask him "Do you think you'll ever get back together?"

"Who knows what the future holds," he replied.

Slowly my heart sank like a wounded battleship.

I was an idiot for telling him that I had been thinking about him. After we got off the phone, I felt like crying. Since meeting him, I knew things would be complicated because he had children, but did not anticipate that his *baby's mama* would put a wedge between us this soon, if at all. Everything was fine until she started to suspect that he was seeing someone else. Though she had a boyfriend, the idea of him dating someone drove her nuts. As more time went by, he texted me less and less and then stopped calling altogether. Even though I had not caused any of the damage, I felt the need to do some sort of damage control.

Three years passed and Butterfly still has not heard from Pinkerton. She would soon be out of money. The matchmaker finds a wealthy prince for her to marry, but she refuses his offer and insists that she was still married to Pinkerton. The matchmaker encourages her to rethink her decision because in Japan, abandonment by a spouse is the equivalent of a divorce. This new wealthy suitor could save Butterfly and her housekeeper, who are now on the brink of financial ruin, but Butterfly refuses the proposal. Even her housekeeper believes that Pinkerton has deserted Butterfly, though she humors her and stands by her side as they pray daily for his return. Even after three years, Butterfly believes that "some day he'll come."

As more time went by, I began to see things differently. Though up until that point, his words said otherwise, I began to feel like the whole time he just used me as a pawn; that he had wanted *his baby's mama* back this whole time and that maybe, I was just the bait that helped him snag her.

I was not entirely sure if he had lost interest in me because she had stolen it or if the only reason he kept talking to me was because he thought he was gonna *get some* when I went down South for work. It had been a while since he called, but he had warned me ahead of time that their cell phones often lost service when they were traveling down the coast. Maybe he had not had phone service, but still, I could not help but notice every time he updated his Facebook status. If he had been on Facebook, he surely could have sent me a quick note, no? *Maybe he was busy.*

To my surprise, he texted me- song lyrics.

You got your ball you've got your chain,

Tied to me tight tie me up again.

Who's got their claws in you my friend.

Into your heart I'll beat again.

Sweet like candy to my soul.

Sweet you rock, sweet you roll.

Lost for you I'm so lost for you.

A few hours later he texted even more.

Maybe you're gonna be the one who saves me.

Oh great, another guy who wants me to save him. It was flattering at least. It gave me a little hope, but I still wondered where he and I stood. Was he seeing someone else on the ship? Should I find someone else myself?

To complicate things, the hedge fund manager continued to pursue me, but I did not know if I should accept his offers. My heart was already set on someone else.

"Go out with the hedge fund manager," my friend pressed.

"I can't, well maybe I could..."

I began to question whether or not it would be ethical to date him. I did not like to date more than one person at a time, but with the sailor being in South Carolina, it only seemed right for me to pursue other *interests* --- unless he wanted to be exclusive, of course. I kept wondering about our exclusivity while trying to politely put off the hedge fund manager, but not lose him completely.

Late one night after a few drinks I finally decided to ask. I dialed his phone, but he did not answer, so I inevitably texted him, "What's up?"

He texted back a few hours later with a thought provoking response, "Not much you?"

This is where I decided to slyly slip in the question that had been on my mind for days, "I was just wondering...are you currently dating anyone else ?"

Nice job.

He texted me back a few minutes later, "...I didn't know we were dating."

Still refusing the matchmaker's offer, Butterfly spends her days and her nights at her window staring at the harbor, hoping that Pinkerton will one day return. Prince Yamadori comes to visit again, seeking her hand in marriage. Though she is disrespectful and rude to him, he still desperately desires to wed her; she is very beautiful. In the meantime, the American Consul pays a visit. He comes to read Butterfly a "Dear John" letter from Pinkerton, who is too cowardly to face her himself.

I wanted to cry. I felt like an innocent maiden, once again, the victim of a another heart-jacking. It seemed that he was not a faithful crew member to the ship, but more so a lowly pirate only after my treasure chest and my booty, who would spin song lyrics for days to get it. I was glad I never kissed him. The only kiss I wanted to give him now was a metaphorical kiss goodbye.

Still not having heard from him, I decided to go to NYC solo to meet a friend for lunch. I parked my car at a garage in Stamford and nervously ran across the street looking over my shoulder as I did, making sure no strangers followed behind. I had never been to The City by myself before.

I purchased a ticket and waited on the Metro North platform. Though the number on the ticket matched up with the one on the platform, I still worried I was on the wrong side in the wrong lane. The train arrived and I took it all the way to Grand Central Terminal. It was something I did it many times before, but this was the first time I did it alone and I was a bit nervous – *well, terrified really.*

Not much was different from all the other times I had arrived at the station. I walked up the stairs past the dingy tunnel that held the tracks and ascended into the terminal. It stood like a shrine that brought together the history and life of Manhattan's past and present creating a timeless existence encased entirely in large bricks of white marble.

I stood in awe for a moment as I always did upon arrival, but this time I stood there mainly because I was unsure of where to go next. All I knew was that somehow I had to find the subway. *Somehow.* As I pondered, I looked up at the ceiling eternally painted midnight blue and adorned with stars and constellations. They looked down at me as if they were the answer to all my navigational questions; the star map that would lead me to the subway and all subsequent stops on my journey.

Eventually, I started to walk. My quick advance towards the exit and inevitable entry onto Lexington Avenue was ignited by the glares of passerby's whose stares made it clear that I looked as obliviously alien as I felt. I looked up one last time to see Pisces and Taurus dance across the plaster sky before I was spit out into the daylight, bright in contrast to the dark concourse.

Reluctantly I searched for the most benign of pedestrians; someone who would not be too annoyed with me for asking for directions. I needed to find the

Shuttle and then the 1 Train, *whatever that meant.* Unsure of the order, a girl, probably a college student patiently explained that I needed to take the Shuttle to Times Square and then catch the 1 Train.

I thanked her and repeated the instructions over and over again in my head in the same way one ties a string to their finger as to not forget. I descended the steps, back to the gray basement. Now I would have to figure out how to get a Metro Card from an automated machine.

A queue of people began to form behind me as I tinkered with the confusing machinery. I put in a five-dollar-bill and it spit out a few quarters and some gold coins. I stepped away from the machine and searched frantically for my ticket. I held the curious coins in one hand wondering what the gold ones were. *I thought they did away with subway tokens years ago...* I looked at them. They were not subway tokens but gold dollars. I didn't even realize in the midst of this transaction that I had the ticket and receipt in my hand the entire time. I swiped my Metro Card and walked through the gates.

Cautiously I moved forward as the music of skilled subway musicians echoed quickly from one end of the corridor to the other as if they had set the entire thing ablaze. It felt like I was on some sort of scavenger hunt. I lit up every time I saw a sign that had a big "S" for Shuttle on it and walked towards it obediently; the same unquestionable sleepwalk of the brainwashed. I never realized how foreign one could feel in their own country; though I was surrounded by signs written in English, an onlooker would have easily pegged me as a traveler from abroad.

During lunch, my cell phone rang. I excitedly grabbed for it nearly knocking over my soda. Finally! I looked at the caller ID and did not recognize the number. It was a Connecticut area code. I debated wether or not I should pick it up. I hated picking up the phone not knowing who was ringing it.

To my surprise, it was the doctor's office calling with my pap results. I became very silent as I nervously awaited the verdict. If I had a disease or the beginning stages of cervical cancer, it surely stemmed from something I acquired from my ex who had probably been cheating on me.

"The pap results were normal. No HPV and everything else was negative. You need to do a retest in six months," she said.

l felt relieved.

That afternoon, when I drove home after leaving The City, it was still light out, a warm summer day. I felt relieved that I made it back to my car and Connecticut safely. Still en route, I noticed that I was approaching the first exit for Bridgeport: the exit that led to one of my favorite sea glass collecting locations: Seaside Park. Suddenly, I got the sudden urge to collect sea glass and veered towards the exit.

When I arrived at the beach's parking lot, I strategically parked in a spot that was not too close to the other people, but also not too far away so they would hear me scream for help should something happen. I had been raped and I was not going to let it happen again.

I walked the breezy beach alone. The sun now hidden behind clouds made it colder than I expected. I thought of him and though I did not hear from him, I pulled my cell out of my pocket and checked my phone just to be sure. No new messages. No missed calls. I looked out towards the sea and wondered if I would ever hear from him again. I imagined his life and what it must be like to live on the ship. I thought that if it worked out, dating a sailor that I met while bartending on a yacht was a very romantic story. Would he come to New York? Was his phone just out of service because they were out at sea? Would he ever call? If it was meant to be it would, I concluded.

Suddenly my phone lit up and started to vibrate in my pocket. I was so thrilled I nearly dropped it into the sand.

"Damn it," I muttered, looking at the caller ID. It was the hedge fund manager.

The hedge fund manager still wanted to take me out. He had texted me several times over the last week, but being love sick over the sailor, I was fairly unresponsive. I texted him back and tried to remain neutral.

When Pinkerton finally returns to Nagasaki after several years, he does not go alone but with his new American wife. He had only used poor naïve Butterfly as a time filler between returning to the US and finding a *real* wife. He never had any intention of getting back together with her.

That day, when the Consul arrives at Butterfly's home, she first asks him, "when do the robins nest in in America?"

He doesn't understand the question, so she explains to him that her husband, Pinkerton, said he would be back when "the robins nest."

"The robins have already nested three times here in Japan," she begins. "Over in America, do they nest less frequently?" she asks him.

The Consul carries on his attempt to give Butterfly the news about Pinkerton. She excitedly misinterprets his words. Instead of being sad, she is is overjoyed that Pinkerton is returning to her. Now the Consul really doesn't have the heart to tell her the truth. He attempts to warn her of the truth, but Butterfly refuses to listen and she presents him with a child: Pinkerton's son.

"His name is Trouble, but when his father returns, he will be called Joy."

She is convinced that when he sees his son they will reunite. The fact that Pinkerton sent the Consul to see her is enough proof of interest to Butterfly.

It was getting colder and windier as the clouds began to completely mask the sun. As a child, I dreamed of finding real treasure on the beach, a pirate's chest or maybe a diamond ring that had fallen from some unfortunate woman's finger. As a kid and even now, I watched enviously as old men spent their afternoons scouring the beach with metal detectors.

I remember a few instances when I was small in which my mother took me downtown to the pawn shop. She did not tell my father where we were going or what she was doing. He would have been very angry. At the pawn shop, she paid the clerk to *once again*, get back her sister's engagement ring. It was not the first time her sister's then husband had stolen and pawned it in order to sustain his heroine addiction.

A cannon fires. Butterfly looks through her telescope and sees that Pinkerton's vessel has arrived. She is convinced he has come back for her and anticipates a joyous reunion. She, the baby, and her housekeeper wait all day for his return. It is nightfall and he has not yet arrived. Everyone but Butterfly has fallen asleep. The housekeeper tells Butterfly to get some rest and offers to wake her when Pinkerton arrives.

Pinkerton and his new wife come for the baby. Without consulting Butterfly, the new wife has already agreed to raise the child. As soon as Pinkerton steps into the house and sees how Butterfly has decorated it for his return, he realizes he has made a huge mistake.

On the beach, I nervously collected the glass, keeping one eye on the sand and the other on the emergency escape route I created in my mind. As I walked through the sand, various cars pulled up and parked along the sidewalk. I felt like the people in them were staring at me, though it was more likely they were just sitting there eating on their lunch breaks. Among the ancient smooth pieces of sea glass I collected, I came upon a fresh jagged shard and picked it up *just in case.* Carefully, I carried it in my hand, and thought about how in an instant, I too could turn that glass on myself if I wanted to.

She happily flies down the stairs expecting to be reunited with her husband, but instead is faced with the reality of the situation, only the new Mrs. Pinkerton and the Consul stand in the room. She agrees to give them what they have come for, her son, but only on one condition: that Pinkerton comes to fetch him.

It was green, hard, and shiny, not soft and smooth like the pieces of real sea glass. I pictured myself using it to stab my faceless attacker as I walked along the damp part of the shore right where the waves stopped; a spot where I often found pieces of glass that were recently uncovered by waves. Though I put up a good front, I secretly wondered if I would be able to do it, even if attacked.

Watching the clock, Butterfly carefully calculates Pinkerton's arrival. She reveals her father's sword and read its inscription "To die with honor when one can no longer live with honor." Within seconds of him approaching, she stabs herself with the blade and crawls over to her son where she dies just as Pinkerton enters the room.

I was shocked by the lack of sea glass I found. Usually I had Ziplock bags full of it, and this time I barely had a fistful. Was it because I wasn't wearing my glasses and it was harder for me to see it? I doubted that was it.

I began to become suspicious and search for it frantically. Where was it? Where was all the sea glass? I looked for it everywhere. Had my ex-boyfriend come during the summer months and stripped the beach of it to spite me? The thought alone upset me. He would do it just to hurt me, take the last of these treasures that were worthless to him only because they meant something to me. Defeated, I drove home and to make matters worse, he still had not called.

The next morning, I awoke from a dream, crying. I dreamt that although I had fallen for him, he had never even liked me. I brushed away my tears as I got out of bed and walked over to my jewelry box. I went through it and pulled out something I had not seen in a while: my engagement ring.

I put it on my right ring finger, not my left because this time I was not playing dress-up. I was not trying to pretend it was something it was not, but no matter what happened in the past or why we broke up, this diamond ring was physical proof that at one time, somebody loved me and I decided that I would hold onto that thought, that feeling until somebody wanted to love me again. What mattered now was that at one time, someone loved me, even if it was just a little.

Though my truck recovered from the vandalism, I still find pieces of glass hidden in between the seats and crevices from time to time. And occasionally, I drive back to West Haven, to look for my past still hoping that something or someone will appear from nothing and no one.

At the end of *Splash,* Madison can no longer exist on land and must return to her home in the ocean. After a tearful goodbye with her loved one, she jumps into the East River as he watches from the dock. It is the ultimate test of love, will he jump into the ocean to be with her, thus leaving behind his life as he has known it and all of his familial relationships? Or will their lives part forever where the land meets the sea? Perhaps one day, I too will find a man who is willing plunge into the depths of the ocean to be with me.

The End

About the Author

Hayley Rose Horzepa is currently working on another book also set in Waterbury, CT. The book debuts later this year. In the meantime, you can read more of her work by subscribing to her blog at HayleysComments.com and following her on Twitter @HroseStudios

Hayley has written for both online and print publications including *The Huffington Post, Gender Across Borders: A Global Feminist Blog, The Republican-American, All Things Healing,* and several others. She has appeared on *BBC TV, Huff Post Live, The Geraldo Rivera Radio Show* and others advocating for women's rights and speaking out about rape.

You can contact the author with any further comments or questions at HRH@HayleysComments.com

To thine own self be true-

44035496R00117

Made in the USA
Middletown, DE
27 May 2017